CHARLES EVANS
8895 THOROLD STONE RD.
NIAGARA FALLS, ONT.
L2E 6S4

Is This the Last Century?

Is This the Last Century?

David Webber and N. W. Hutchings

THOMAS NELSON PUBLISHERS
Nashville

Third printing

Copyright © 1979 by David Webber and N. W. Hutchings

All rights reserved under International and Pan-American Conventions. Published in Nashville, Tennessee, by Thomas Nelson Inc., Publishers and simultaneously in Don Mills, Ontario, by Thomas Nelson & Sons (Canada) Limited. Manufactured in the United States of America.

All Bible verses are taken from the King James Version of the Bible.

Library of Congress Cataloging in Publication Data

Webber, David.
   Is this the last century?

   1. End of the world. 2. Twentieth century—Forecasts. I. Hutchings, Noah W., joint author. II. Title.
BT876.W42   236′.3   79-16968
ISBN 0-8407-5701-8

Contents

	Introduction vii
One	Jesus Is Coming 9
Two	A Prophetic Calendar 34
Three	The Budding Fig Tree 52
Four	Elijah Must Come 61
Five	Nations in the Net 74
Six	Russia: Enemy to the North 86
Seven	The Mystery of Babylon 103
Eight	The Parade of Planets 120
Nine	Mark of the Beast 134
Ten	The Last Century 141

Introduction

Are we living in the last century?

This vital question affects every man, woman, boy, and girl living today. This awesome possibility looms ominously on the human horizon and confronts each of the more than four billion people on this planet. A time of unparalleled affliction, tyranny, and destruction must occur before the most shattering event in all the history of man occurs—the physical return of Jesus Christ to the earth in real, visible, and overwhelming power.

The evidence of prophetic Scripture points to the possibility of Christ's return by the end of this century. For the non-Christian residents of our globe there is, with rare exception, a claustrophobic feeling of helpless inescapability, of hopeless inevitability. It is "almost solid gloom and disaster," according to syndicated columnist Jack McArthur. This foreboding affects those in high and low stations in life—the famous as well as the obscure. Hollywood superstar Barbra Streisand has secluded herself from society, explaining that "The state of the world so frightens me!" While many do not seclude themselves, nonetheless they are of the same opinion.

With the first serious attempt at a negotiated peace between Israel and Egypt threatened by hostility from other Arab nations, and with Russia and China teetering on the brink of war and the Middle East in turmoil, the world is swiftly moving toward its rendezvous with destiny—the coming of Israel's Messiah to overrule and abolish the Antichrist, roll back the Tribulation tides of evil, and establish Jesus' righteous rule from Jerusalem.

One

Jesus Is Coming

Jesus is coming!

The literal return of our living Lord is very near. We believe that signs in the earth and the heavens, signs outlined in God's Word, lead to the inescapable conclusion that Jesus Christ is coming to the earth again soon.

Throughout history men have looked anxiously for the second coming of Christ. The promise of His return has been a driving, motivating force among believers from the beginning of church history. The first disciples were convinced that Jesus would return soon. Paul called that promised return the "blessed hope" of the Christian. In every generation since Pentecost, the children of God—those born into God's family through faith in Jesus Christ—have lived with the constant expectation that their Savior might return at any moment. In each of the past nineteen centuries there have been believers who were confident that theirs could be the final century of man's history. Yet each century has come and gone. Scoffers have asked, "Where is the promise of his coming?" (2 Pet. 3:4) for nearly two millennia. How, then, can we say with such confidence that Jesus is coming, and how can we be so certain that He is coming soon?

The answer to these questions is seen daily in the world around us. The prophecies of God's Word are being fulfilled with miraculous accuracy. Each generation since Pentecost has had the promise of the Lord's return, but ours is the first to see a multitude of signs point so dramatically to the event. The Old Testament prophets, the New Testament writers, and Jesus Himself gave us scores of clues, legions of guideposts, and multitudes of signs that point to the second coming of Jesus Christ. Ours is the first generation to see these signs come together in an ever-sharpening focus. We are the first believers to whom the distant and often obscure prophecies of Christ's return are as timely as this morning's newspaper.

How can we be so certain Jesus is coming soon? A traveler knows he is approaching a town when he sees an increase in the number of road signs, billboards, houses, businesses, and other indications of urban life. God's Word has set forth an impressive array of billboards and road signs that point to Christ's return. We are to look for these signs as we journey. For the first time in history the roadside is literally cluttered with them. Every day brings into view more and more of these biblical billboards. The message is clear: Jesus is coming soon.

In this chapter and throughout this book we will see what the Word of God has to say concerning the signs of Jesus Christ's second coming. The Bible speaks to four basic groups on this very important matter: to the nation of Israel; to the saved, the true church of Jesus Christ; to the apostate church, those who profess Christianity but have not genuinely received Christ as Savior and Lord; and to the unsaved, those who have never trusted Christ.

First, listen to Christ's words to Israel:

> Therefore be ye also ready: for in such an hour as ye think not the Son of man cometh. . . . Blessed is that servant, whom his lord when he cometh shall find so doing (Matt. 24:44,46).

To the saved the message is:

> And when these things begin to come to pass, then look up, and lift up your heads; for your redemption draweth nigh. . . . So likewise ye, when ye see these things come to pass, know ye that the kingdom of God is nigh at hand (Luke 21:28,31).
>
> But ye, brethren, are not in darkness, that that day should overtake you as a thief (1 Thess. 5:4).

Of the apostate church the Bible says:

> . . . they received not the love of the truth, that they might be saved. And for this cause God shall send them strong delusion, that they should believe a lie: That they all might be damned who believed not the truth, but had pleasure in unrighteousness (2 Thess. 2:10–12).
>
> . . . there shall come in the last days scoffers, walking after their own lusts, And saying, Where is the promise of his coming? for since the fathers fell

asleep, all things continue as they were from the beginning of the creation (2 Pet. 3:3,4).

The Scriptures also speak of the unsaved in general, saying:

> ... the day of the Lord so cometh as a thief in the night. For when they shall say, Peace and safety; then sudden destruction cometh upon them, as travail upon a woman with child; and they shall not escape (1 Thess. 5:2,3).

The Word of God is clear. No person or group is left out. There can be no excuse for ignorance concerning the second coming of Christ. God addresses Himself to all people, giving us signs indicating the nearness of His Son's return. We will begin our study by looking briefly at fifteen important signs that are signals to all people. They are arranged in five divisions: (1) The Segregation of Man, (2) The Problems of Man, (3) The Empires of Man, (4) The Wisdom of Man, and (5) The Society of Man.

The Segregation of Man

The Bible's prophetic passages divide mankind into three main categories: Israel, the Gentile nations, and the church. God considers those who have trusted Jesus Christ to be a distinct group, separate both from Israel and from the Gentile nations, even though the church includes people of both Jewish and Gentile stock. For the purposes of this prophetic discussion, when we speak of the church we will on occasion include the apostate church as well.

Let us consider each of these three groups in turn to determine if the current pattern of events conforms to the signs set forth in biblical prophecy.

Israel

The main sign in the Bible announcing the beginning of the last days is the return of the Jewish remnant to Palestine and the establishment of Israel as a nation. This return is prophesied in Ezekiel 36:24: "I will take you from among the heathen, and gather you out of all countries, and will bring you into your own land." According to Ezekiel 38:8, the return of the remnant was to take place in "the latter years." Almost every book in the Old Testament, and at least half the books in the New Testament, point to the Jews as God's timepiece for Christ's return.

The modern exodus began in earnest after World War II when European Jews, sickened and discouraged by the annihilation of six million of their number by Hitler, returned to their ancient homeland. There they hoped to live out their lives in peace and security. In the meantime, the Arab nations of Africa and Asia began to persecute the Jewish populations within their borders.

An Nahar, an Arab publication in Beirut, reported: "The Jews of Arab states were driven out of their ancient home. . . . They were shamefully deported after their property had been commandeered or taken over at the lowest possible valuation." Jewish emigration from Arab nations is reported in the 1976 edition of *Myths and Facts:*

	Jewish Population 1948	Jewish Population 1976
Egypt	75,000	350
Libya	40,000	20
Iraq	125,000	400
Syria	45,000	4,000
Lebanon	20,000	1,000
Yemen	61,000	0
Tunisia	110,000	2,000
Morocco	300,000	20,000
Algeria	150,000	500

Another biblical sign concerning Israel in the latter years is the alignment of her chief enemies: Gog to the north (Ezek. 38:1,2); the surrounding nations of Iran (biblical Persia), Ethiopia, Libya, and Turkey (Ezek. 38:5,6); and Eastern Europe (Ezek. 38:6). All nations will be aligned against Israel at the time of our Lord's return (Zech. 14:1,2). Even now we see Israel with one wavering ally—the United States—and a fragile negotiated peace with Egypt.

Another important sign in Israel is the building of a temple. In accordance with Daniel 9:27, Matthew 24:15, 2 Thessalonians 2:4, and Revelation 11, Israel must construct a building that will serve as a temple before the Lord's return. The Antichrist must profess himself to be the promised Messiah in the Jewish temple in Jerusalem.

Jews are now allowed to pray on the temple site for the first time in over 1,900 years. Young boys from the tribe of Levi are being trained in temple services, including the offering of animal sacrifices. Work is nearing completion on a building called the Great Synagogue, one mile west of the former temple site. This building will contain all the important articles of furniture that were in the old temple, including the Ark of the Covenant. If political conditions continue to prevent building the temple on the original plot of ground now occupied by the Dome of the Rock, the Great Synagogue could serve as the Tribulation temple.

According to Daniel 9:27, the Antichrist will bring political peace to the Middle East by enacting a seven-year covenant between Israel and her enemies—probably the Arab nations. Such a covenant has been in existence for several years, although Israel has not signed it. The Arab nations have adopted a "Palestinian National Covenant," an agreement they insist Israel must sign in order to buy peace with the Moslem world. *Myths and Facts* for 1976 reports: "The use of the word 'covenant' rather than 'charter' reflects the supposed national sanctity of the document."

According to Bible prophecy, conditions in Israel are right for the appearance of the Antichrist, the man of sin who will be destroyed at the glorious coming of our great God and Savior, Jesus Christ (2 Thess. 2:8).

Gentile Nations

In Luke 21:23,24 Jesus prophesied that Israel would be scattered to all nations and persecuted "until the times of the Gentiles be fulfilled." During the present age, Gentiles have ruled the earth. God has been calling Gentiles to faith in Jesus Christ so that they can inherit heavenly glory (Acts 15:16,17). The fullness of the Gentiles during the time, or dispensation, of grace was foretold in Noah's blessing upon Japheth (Gen. 9:27).

However, in accordance with Joel 3:10–16 and many other Scripture passages, Gentile nations will continue to beat their plowshares into swords and arm themselves with massive weapons of destruction. In 1950, the total international arms business amounted to $200 million. Today the international arms traffic has risen to over $400 billion each year.

Jesus said that after Israel reclaimed the old city of Jerusalem (a prophecy that was fulfilled in 1967), the Gentiles could only look forward to distress, perplexity, and destruction, for their time would soon run out. Zechariah 12, Revelation 16:16, Joel 3, and Revelation 19:11–21 inform us without qualification that the armies of all nations will be destroyed upon the plains of Megiddo (Armageddon), and that the flesh of those who die there will be eaten by birds. In Matthew 24:28, Jesus called these birds "eagles."

Michael Estes, a converted rabbi, stated in his book *Next Visitor to Planet Earth,* "The vultures are already circling in the Valley of Armageddon. God's preparing a feast for seven months for these vultures to feed upon. And a new breed of vulture has appeared in Israel, a breed never seen before. These vultures are multiplying at three times the normal rate in Israel. This is a sign of the end time." We have

The Church

The church is the third division of mankind the Bible deals with in conjunction with the latter days. The strict definition of the church is "a called-out body of worshipers of God." Through the dispensation of God's grace—the Church Age—the church as an organizational shelter has included both true and false believers. In 1 Thessalonians 4 and 5 Paul writes of the true Christians, who will be taken out of the world prior to the Tribulation. In 2 Thessalonians 1 and 2, Paul makes reference to pseudo-believers. These people will be left when the Bridegroom comes for the true bride. These false church members will form the Tribulation church, the harlot of the Antichrist system.

A recent newspaper headline read: "World Council of Churches Votes to Support Terrorists in Africa." The WCC has actually sent financial aid to the Soviet-backed guerrilla forces that have slaughtered hundreds and perhaps thousands of civilians in the name of African liberation. Their tactics, which have brought death to both white and black citizens, range from slashing the throats of black citizens who try to participate in elections to shooting down civilian-operated airliners with Russian-made antiaircraft missiles.

Time magazine reported that the WCC has excused Russian aggression while condemning South Africa and the United States, two of the few nations left in the world where freedom of religion still exists. Meanwhile, socialization and political indoctrination of churches in the United States and abroad continues. More and more, the church sees itself as an agency for social action rather than an organism dedicated to spiritual matters.

All the signs indicate that conditions in the modern church are ripe for the appearance of a modern political messiah, one who will promise to socialize the world. When he appears, the false churches of the world will be ready to worship him.

The Problems of Man

The three major physical problems of the human race have been the same throughout recorded history: war, disease, and famine.

War

The first sign in this part of our study is war. Jesus said in Matthew 24:6,7 that there would be wars and rumors of wars, nation rising against nation and kingdom against kingdom. Consider these grisly statistics.

In the Russo-Japanese War of 1904–05 there were 130,000 casualties. A total of 162,000 were killed in the Balkan Wars of 1912–13. There were 431,000 killed in the Spanish Civil War. The Colombian Civil War claimed 200,000 from 1948–53. Approximately 581,000 died in the Korean War. World War I saw the horrifying figure of 10,000,000 casualties, surpassed only by the 50,000,000 of World War

II.* Add to these figures the vast numbers, both military and civilian, who were killed in the Vietnam and African wars.

Statistics indicate that during the past 5,000 years of recorded history, some 600,000,000 men, women, and children have died in war. One half of that total casualty figure can be accounted for in the twentieth century alone.

The increase in the number of wars, along with the rise in casualties suffered in modern warfare, is another sign that we are living in the latter days.

Disease

In Matthew 24:7, Jesus listed pestilence as a sign of the end of the age and His impending return. These are probably epidemic diseases. For years, modern medical science has been hailed as the miracle that would usher in the millennium on earth, allowing men and women to live at least one hundred years in good health and prosperity.

It just has not happened that way. Processed foods, man's changing life-style, and the so-called new morality have produced increased heart trouble, cancer, and venereal disease epidemics. In addition, there is now evidence to suggest that modern drugs may have become a mirage rather than the miracle they are acclaimed to be.

In a 1976 segment of the Public Broadcast System's television program *Nova*, prominent

---

*See Salem Kirban and Gary C. Cohen, *Revelation Visualized* (Huntington, Pa.: Kirban Inc.), p. 142, for these statistics.

physicians from the United States and Great Britain were interviewed. It was their consensus that antibiotics could someday become ineffective because many germs are developing immunities to the drugs. And in developing immunities, these germ strains are becoming stronger and more difficult to combat. The physicians concluded that within a few years medical science could be back in the Dark Ages as far as fighting plagues and disease epidemics is concerned.

If this dark prediction becomes a reality, and according to prophecy it will, then crowded urban areas such as New York, Los Angeles, Chicago, Tokyo, and Moscow will become death traps.

Famine

Famine is caused most often by changing weather patterns. We know from Joel 1:15–20, Matthew 24:7, and Revelation 11 that the last days will be characterized by storms and droughts that will cause the worst famine the world has ever seen. If we are living near the end of the age, as the signs indicate, then we must also be very near to this predicted catastrophe. Some thirty nations around the earth's equatorial belt have already experienced severe drought.

England usually receives more rain than she needs. Yet in 1976, the nation experienced the greatest drought in 250 years. Joel prophesied that in the last days the great rivers of the earth would dry up. The headlines in England's May 18, 1976, newspapers announced that the drought had left the Thames a dry riverbed. Pleasure yachts and boats of

Jesus Is Coming

all kinds rested on the mud at the bottom of this once-great river. Lakes and reservoirs that provide water for the English people were from one-half to two-thirds empty.

The drought there has ended, but its very occurrence illustrates how quickly such events can cripple a nation. Certainly there have always been droughts and famines, but with the present explosive population growth there are billions of city dwellers who depend on grain and meat produced in rural areas. The stage is being set for the most horrible famine the world has ever known.

For further evidence connected with the sign of famine in the last days, we refer to an article by Roscoe Drummond: "CIA'S World Weather Forecast Pictures Major Disasters." This article appeared in the May 11, 1976, edition of the *St. Paul Dispatch:*

> No nation anywhere in the world, especially Russia, China, India, and the United States, can afford to take lightly the ominous . . . century weather forecast covering the entire planet and prepared for the CIA. . . . It is a calmly chilling and scholarly meteorological study pointing to such radical changes in the climate as to cause its authors to warn that . . . the consequences in political and economic upheaval and international violence will be "almost beyond human comprehension" . . . . It would be perilous to assume that its report is misjudging the oncoming weather that every continent will be experiencing during the rest of the 20th century and during the lifetimes of every human being on this planet . . . . Its imperative is human survival

without such frustration and fear that war becomes inevitable because of massive starvation and death .... Over vast areas of the earth's land mass, that even now cannot produce enough food to feed all mankind, the signs now accumulating point to these forecasts: There will be destructive droughts where droughts have not been occurring. The climatic changes that have taken place during the past five years can, the experts are convinced, bring consequences such as the following: The Soviet Union ... would lose the lush wheat fields of the entire Kazakhstan. China would experience a major famine .... Droughts would grip India ... resulting in starvation for 150 million people. Canada would lose fifty per cent of its productive capacity. Europe's food exports would drop to zero. The United States would be least affected ... but with food shortages stalking the whole world, the United States could provide only marginal and selective assistance. ...

Jesus listed famine as one of the signs of His return. We read of this dire prophecy in the Old Testament also:

Alas for the day! for the day of the Lord is at hand, and as a destruction from the Almighty shall it come .... The seed is rotten under their clods ... the barns are broken down; for the corn is withered. How do the beasts groan! the herds of cattle are perplexed, because they have no pasture .... The beasts of the field cry also unto thee: for the rivers of waters are dried up ... (Joel 1:15–20).

Jesus also said in Matthew 24:7 that one of the signs of His return would be an increase in earthquakes in various places. A quick glance at the latest issue of the *World Almanac* will verify that earthquakes are increasing. During the Tribulation there will be earthquakes of such proportions that the Bible says every wall will fall to the ground and islands will sink into the oceans (Ezek. 38:20; Rev. 16:18). Astronomers John Gribbin and Stephen Plagemann have predicted that at the next alignment of the planets, which will occur in 1982, massive gravitational pull from the sun and planets could set off a rash of earthquakes. Some might even be so intense, they claim, as to split California along the San Andreas fault. (More about this in Chapter 8.) As we consider the prospects, we cannot help but be reminded that the coming of Jesus Christ is near.

The Empires of Man

Jesus Christ said that in the last days kingdom would rise against kingdom. Since World War II, the international political scene has been dominated by power-bloc politics and economics. Only in recent months have we seen this system begin to show cracks and weaknesses. Such a reshuffling is necessary to make way for the worldwide government of the Antichrist. Nevertheless, for the past two decades we have witnessed world politics taking the form of an international balancing act between the Communist bloc, the free-world bloc (including the Common Market and the United States), and the Third-World bloc. Let us see what the Bible has to say about these empires of man as they will exist in the last days.

The Common Market

The time of Gentile world empires, as relating to Gentile control over Jerusalem and the land of Palestine, dates back to ancient Babylon—approximately 600 B.C. Nebuchadnezzar, king of Babylon, had visions of a perpetual world empire. God answered the king's delusions of grandeur with a miraculous dream. In this dream Nebuchadnezzar saw a large image of a ruler, composed of four metals from the head down to the feet: gold, silver, brass, and iron. Only Daniel could interpret the dream, and his interpretation has been verified by history.

The gold head was Babylon. The breast and arms of silver were Medo-Persia. The belly and thighs of brass represented Greece. The legs of iron and the feet of iron and clay pictured Rome. According to Daniel 2:40,41, the last empire would be divided—not destroyed, as some have suggested.

Even though the segments of the last empire would war against each other, Daniel's prophecy indicates that the last vestiges of that Roman empire would be very much in evidence when the Messiah comes to establish His eternal kingdom on the earth. With the breaking up of Roman rule, the pieces of that empire—Spain, England, Belgium, the Netherlands, Germany, Portugal, France, and Italy—still controlled the world through their vast colonial empires. After World War II, these empires broke apart, leaving only relatively small chunks of iron mixed among the clay nations (Dan. 2:42,43).

The prophecy further stated that in the days

before Christ's return ten of these nations would form an alliance. Of these ten nations it is recorded in Daniel 2:44: "And in the days of these kings shall the God of heaven set up a kingdom, which shall never be destroyed. . . ."

When the headquarters for the Common Market was built in Brussels, ten flagpoles were erected in front of the structure. The tenth place was filled in January, 1980, when Greece joined the Common Market.

An editorial in the October, 1975, edition of *The European Community,* the official publication of the Common Market, stated in part, "The EEC Rome Treaty supports the interpretation of the books of Ezekiel, Daniel, and Revelation that this 'last-days' kingdom is a new Roman Empire." If, as it seems, the Common Market is the alliance mentioned by Daniel, we cannot be far removed from the second coming of Jesus Christ.

The October, 1977, edition of *European Community* correctly guessed that Greece would become the tenth member of the alliance before the end of 1980. The prophesied ten-headed union is here.

The Communist Nations

Ezekiel prophesied that in the latter days a great and powerful nation would rise up to the north of Jerusalem and form an alliance with many of the present-day Arab nations against Israel. In Ezekiel 38:1,2, this northern power is called Gog, the land of Meshech and Tubal. Many reliable commentaries agree that Gog is Russia; Meshech is Moscow, the capital of the old western division of the land; and Tubal is Tobolsk, the capital of the old eastern division. A recent issue of *Soviet Life* carried an article on the revival of Tobolsk as the result of an oil boom there. The city has become second only to Moscow in importance to Russia's continued development.

The Communist grip on China and much of Asia is also indicated in prophecy. Revelation 9:16 states that an army of 200 million horsemen will march from the east and cross the dry Euphrates River on its way to Armageddon. In our lifetime we have heard the late Chinese leader Mao Tse-tung boast that China could field an army of 200 million men—the exact number mentioned in Revelation. This statement takes on new significance when we realize that by the best available estimates, the entire population of the world was only 250 million when the prophecy was written. Only God could have led John to record what must have seemed at the time to be a ridiculously high number. In addition, with the completion of the Euphrates Dam at Tabqa, Syria, the Euphrates can be dried up on command for the first time in history. This is just another sign that we are living in the last days.

Another interesting aspect of the Communist advance is seen in Europe. Nearly every country of western Europe has a strong Communist party. Communists have won election to major government positions in Italy and France. If the trend continues, the Common Market nations will be forced to choose between a non-Communist dictatorship or total Communist rule. Under the current political system the Communists are ready to take over all of the Common Market one nation at a time. Faced with this possibility, it is not unreasonable to suggest that free Europe would choose a benevolent dictator over the Marxist alternative. This may be the very decision predicted in Revelation 17:13: "These [possibly referring to the ten kingdoms of the old Roman Empire] have one mind, and shall give their power and strength unto the beast."

The Third-World Bloc

The Third-World nations can probably be identified with the leopard empire of Daniel 7:6,7. When Gog moves against Israel, as predicted in Daniel 7 and Ezekiel 38 and 39, God will defeat them on the mountains of Israel. With the fall of this great power (almost certainly Russia), there will be a political and military vacuum in that part of the world. The leopard empire, which will include the Arab nations, will rapidly expand to fill that power vacuum. Independent and loosely organized, these nations will be easily amalgamated into the Antichrist's one-world government (Rev. 13:1,2,8).

We may divide the Arab nations in the Third-World bloc into two categories, based on their relationship to Israel. The inner six—Syria, Jordan, Lebanon, Iraq, Egypt, and Saudi Arabia—are not mentioned in the accounts of war recorded in Ezekiel 38. We cannot be certain why these nations will not be involved in that great war. It may be that they will have been either conquered or destroyed in a smaller, regional war. In fact, such a war might provide Russia with the very excuse it needs to launch a full-scale invasion.

In spite of Israeli denials, many feel quite strongly that Israel has developed some type of nuclear arms. Her conventional military prowess is well known. So it is not difficult to picture a regional war in which Israel, whether on its own initiative or as a response to an Arab attack, could gain a military victory over the inner six nations. This prospect becomes more plausible in light of Ezekiel's earlier prophecy that Egypt would be so contaminated that not even a dog would be able to live there for forty years (Ezek. 29:10–12).

When Russia unleashes her fury on Israel, she will be joined by the outer four Arab nations—Turkey (biblical Togarmah), Libya, Ethiopia, and Iran (biblical Persia). Ethiopia was once one of the United States' strongest African allies, but Soviet expansionism in the Horn of Africa has almost totally reversed that situation.

For four decades Iran was the non-Communist world's first line of defense against Russian aggression into the Middle East. She was armed with the best weapons the West had to offer. Yet in less than a year's time, the shah of Iran and his Peacock Throne were toppled by forces from within, forces that included at least 25,000 armed Marxist troops. In the confusion that followed the military victory, these Communist soldiers began demanding a significant role in the Iranian government.

No serious student of recent history will suppose for a moment that Russia will allow the political upheaval in Iran to subside without taking advantage of this opportunity to increase Communist influence in that oil-rich country. The only real question is whether the Soviet advance will be political, military, or both.

There are several other smaller Arab nations and some larger ones, like Morocco, far removed from Israel, that evidently do not figure in prophecy.

The development of the Common Market, the growth of the Communist bloc, and the ever-shifting balance of power among the Third-World nations are all in keeping with Bible prophecy. These events are but another very definite sign that we are living near the end of this age.

The Wisdom of Man

The fourth division of our study deals with the wisdom of man, as opposed to the wisdom of God, in the last days. Daniel 12:4 tells us that at the ". . . time of the end: many shall run to and fro, and knowledge shall be increased."

Accelerated Travel

Ours is the most mobile society in history. Daniel said that people in the last days would run to and fro. Until the turn of the twentieth century, most people did not do much traveling. When they did, they were still jogging along on a train or horse at about forty miles per hour. Adam could do nearly that well on one of the animals in the Garden of Eden. However, with the dawn of the twentieth century, man began to travel faster and more often. It is not unusual now for families to travel across the state, nation, or even the world. The average American family moves several times, often from state to state. Jet airplanes often travel 1000 miles per hour. Spacecraft carry men into outer space at speeds in excess of 18,000 miles per hour.

Increase of Knowledge

Daniel also said that knowledge would increase. It has done so at a rate unsurpassed in recorded history. Man fought with swords and bows for 3,500 years before he invented gunpowder. In only a few centuries he advanced from crude handguns to sophisticated weaponry. In the last fifty years he has gone from field artillery to multi-warhead intercontinental ballistic missiles that carry thermonuclear weapons capable of raining total destruction over vast areas at a moment's notice.

In the educational field it is estimated that total world knowledge doubles every two and a half years. Computer science has mushroomed. A computer that would have cost hundreds of thousands of dollars and filled several floors of a large building only twenty years ago can now be purchased for less than two hundred dollars and carried to the office in a coat pocket. Advances in the computer field are coming so rapidly that technology is unable to keep pace. Some computers are actually becoming obsolete before they can be built.

Communications

In Jesus' time it required several months to send a letter from Jerusalem to Rome and receive a reply.

Jesus Is Coming

Only one hundred years ago it still took six months to send and receive correspondence from many portions of the globe. Under these conditions the seven-year Tribulation period would be over before the Antichrist could circulate his various decrees to the rulers of the nations. But now radio, television, and satellite relay communications make it possible for the prophecies of the Revelation to be fulfilled. Everyone throughout the world will see the Antichrist as he stands in the temple. Everyone will see the bodies of the two witnesses as they lie in the streets of Jerusalem. Above all, it is now possible to proclaim the gospel to all the world as Jesus foretold in Matthew 24:14.

The Society of Man

Finally, we must consider several social developments that signal the approach of our Lord's return.

Population Explosion

Jesus said that conditions in the days before His return would be similar to the world situation in Noah's day. One of the major characteristics of Noah's time was population growth (Gen. 6:1). It took nearly 1,900 years for the world population to grow from 250 to 1 billion. In the last 120 years our population has gone from 1 billion to more than 4 billion. Many expect that figure to reach 7 billion by the end of this century.

Lawlessness

According to Jesus, iniquity will abound in the days just prior to His return. Paul wrote in 2 Thessalonians that iniquity, or lawlessness, would be unrestrained in the days surrounding the appearance of the Antichrist. Genesis 6 says that in Noah's time crime and violence filled the earth. That pattern is repeating itself. *Time* magazine reported in June, 1975: "Since 1961, the rate for all serious crimes has more than doubled. . . . Violent crime has had an even sharper increase. In the past 14 years, the rate for robberies has increased 255 per cent, forcible rape 143 per cent, and murder 106 per cent. . . . Of all crime statistics, homicide figures are the most reliable; a body count—more than 20,000 in 1974—shows that Americans are killing each other in wholesale lots." The FBI reports that in the past three years the total crime rate has moderated. However, crime continues to grow, especially violent crimes.

Economics

The Bible projects worldwide inflation at the time of the Tribulation period. The intricate emergency solution to this economic distress will be a system requiring all people to be numbered and to display that number when buying, selling, and working (Rev. 6:5,6; 13:16–18). The one who will control this system, the Antichrist, will have such power through this economic stranglehold that he will be able to demand and receive worship. Even now we are experiencing inflation that is unparalleled by anything in recent history.

Of even greater significance is the trend toward electronic money. The banking industry is moving us closer to a cashless and checkless society in which all purchases and monetary exchanges are carried out by computer. Such a system, as innocent as it may be in concept and design, is tailor-made for the Antichrist.

In Summary

Events and conditions all around us foretell the soon return of Jesus Christ. The Segregation of Man, the Problems of Man, the Empires of Man, the Wisdom of Man, and the Society of Man are all signs. However, nowhere in the Bible are Christians instructed to climb to some mountaintop and wait for His appearance. Instead, in 1 Thessalonians 5, Paul instructs believers in the last days to work and witness, rejoicing in and anticipating the blessed hope. We must keep busy in the Master's work during these last hours before His coming. As one missionary has stated, "We have all eternity to celebrate our victories, and but one short hour before sunset to win them."

TWO
A Prophetic Calendar

Jesus said, "But of that day and hour knoweth no man, no, not the angels of heaven, but my Father only" (Matt. 24:36).

If we are to understand Christ's statement, we must view it from the context in which it was spoken and the times that prompted it. When Jesus stood with His disciples following His resurrection, they asked Him if He would at that time establish His kingdom on earth. He replied, "It is not for you to know the times or the seasons" (Acts 1:7). But the Scriptures are clear that Christians living in the last days can know that Christ's coming is near, even at the door (Matt. 24:33). He rebuked the Pharisees and called them hypocrites because they were able to forecast the weather by looking at the sky, but were unable to recognize Him from Old Testament prophecies (Matt. 16:3).

There is another set of hypocrites in existence today. They scoff at the thought of Christ's return and scorn those who attempt to identify the signs of

A Prophetic Calendar

His coming. Peter warned us that such men would come, and he called them ignorant (2 Pet. 3:3–5).

But can we know? Is there a way we can discern the time of Christ's second coming? The Greek word Jesus chose to use, in saying that those men of His day could not know, is *oida*. It means to know intuitively. A few verses earlier, when He said some could know that His coming was so near as to be at the door, Jesus used the word *ginosko*. This word involves knowing as the result of investigation. Neither Peter nor John nor any of the disciples could know intuitively when Jesus would return. Neither could the angels. That special knowledge was reserved for the Father alone.

Neither could the disciples know the time of Christ's return by investigation. The signs of His return were not available for investigation in their day. Jesus, however, indicated that when the signs He listed did begin appearing, the believers who saw them could know by investigation that His coming was near, even at the door.

We recently toured the Kennedy Space Center and were impressed by a statement from our guide. He said it was the consensus of the scientists who worked and visited there that nothing short of a miracle could prevent man from destroying himself by the year 2000. Clare Booth Luce, who calls herself an optimist, stated, "There is a great likelihood of nuclear war in the next twenty-five years." Is the end so near? Could Jesus return by A.D. 2000?

For the sake of clarity, we should define some

terms used in connection with the second coming of Christ. In order to understand the prophecies that point toward Christ's return, we need to understand the actual events that will surround His coming and the order in which they will occur.

We are currently living in an era commonly called the dispensation of grace. This is the period following the earthly ministry of Christ in which God has temporarily turned His attention from the national interests of Israel so that He can call out from among the Gentiles an assembly of redeemed people—the church. Sometimes this period is referred to as the Church Age.

Toward the end of the Church Age, God will begin preparing Israel to assume once again the exalted position she held under David and Solomon. Although Israel has been scattered as a punishment for her repeated sins, God has not forgotten her altogether. Prophecy says that the Jews will be gathered into Palestine again and prepared by the heavenly Father to receive Jesus as King. This regathering has already begun.

The final seven years of Israel's preparation is called the Tribulation period. It will be a time of severe national and political testing for the Jews. The last three and one-half years of this Tribulation period is called the Great Tribulation, or the Time of Jacob's Trouble. It will be especially severe. In fact, the only thing that will prevent the entire nation of Israel from being destroyed will be the literal return of Christ to defeat the armies of this world at Armageddon. Following this return a temple will be built for Him in Jerusalem, and He will reign over the entire world for a thousand years. This thousand-year period is called the Millennium.

Where, then, do we who are not of the nation of Israel fit into the overall picture? Recall that during this present age God is calling out a people, the church, to be the bride of His Son and co-rulers with Jesus. The Church Age will culminate in an event theologians call the Rapture. As it is described in 1 Thessalonians 4:13–17, the Lord Himself will descend from heaven with a shout. The trumpet of God will sound. The dead in Christ will rise from their graves, and those of us who have trusted Christ during the Church Age will be caught up into the air with the resurrected saints. This event will occur quickly, in the twinkling of an eye. (It should be noted that although the actual word rapture is not found in Scripture, it means "a catching away with ecstasy." The term is used to describe the catching away, or translation, of the completed church.)

When the Church Age believers are safely removed, God will allow the Antichrist to rise to power. He will be the evil ruler and master politician of the Tribulation period. He will persecute Israel and, in his arrogance, challenge the authority of God. This man of sin will lead the ill-fated forces of the world in the battle of Armageddon.

Thus, the order of events will be as follows: (1) the appearance of the signs of Christ's return, especially the regathering of Israel into Palestine; (2) the removal, or rapture, of the Church-Age believers; (3) the appearance of the Antichrist; (4) the seven years of the Tribulation, the latter half of which is called the Time of Jacob's Trouble; (5) the mobilization of the Antichrist's military forces at Armageddon in preparation to annihilate Israel; (6) the return of Christ to defeat the Antichrist and rescue Israel; and (7) the establishment of the millennial kingdom under the direct personal reign of Jesus Christ.

It is important to understand that when Jesus and the prophets spoke of His return, they were speaking of that day when He would come to defeat the Antichrist and establish His earthly kingdom. All the current signs of the times point to that event. Since the saints of the Church Age will be removed before the Tribulation and the final fulfillment of these signs, we can be confident that as we see the signs of His glorious return we are very near the day when we will be caught up in the air to meet Jesus. The implication is plain. If Jesus' coming is near, then the rapture of the Church-Age believers is at least seven years nearer.

Having outlined the order of coming events and defined the important terms involved, let us consider the vital evidence that Christ's return is near.

The Bible tells us that everything God performs is perfect in number (Job 28:25; Ps. 147:4; Isa. 40:26; Luke 12:7). Nothing in God's Word is insignificant, including numbers. God's perfect number is seven, as established in creation. The pattern of sevens is woven into the fabric of Scripture from Genesis to Revelation. God's plan and purpose for the earth and the human race began in the first seven days and is completed in the seventh seal of the Revelation. God

A Prophetic Calendar 39

created man on the sixth day, and six is the number of man (Rev. 13:18).

All through history man has had dominion over the earth. Although He has intervened from time to time, God has allowed man to sow (and reap accordingly) from the very beginning. He has allowed man to make his own choices and to live with the consequences of those choices.

Prophecy, however, speaks of a "day of the Lord" (Isa. 2:12; Joel 2:1; Zech. 14:1; 2 Pet. 3:10). The Bible does not speak of *days* of the Lord, but of the *day* of the Lord. It is mentioned in the singular, yet described in prophecy as extending for some thousand years (Rev. 20:1-6). This is not inconsistent with other passages that teach us that a thousand years, as judged by men, is as one day to God (Ps. 90:4; 2 Pet. 3:8). When this day of the Lord comes, man will no longer dominate. God will reign and everyone will know it.

Many Bible chronologies place the creation of man in the year 4004 B.C., with four years allowed for calendar error. Jesus Christ, the second Adam, was born 4,000 years later. Four in the Bible is the number of the world. Jesus came to save the world (John 3:17). Jesus was born in the "fulness of time" (Gal. 4:4), a term that suggests an exact foreordained date. He was not born in the fullness of the world, the fullness of sin, or the fullness of men. The emphasis is on time. Likewise, we are also told that His return will occur in "the fulness of times" (Eph. 1:9,10).

God deals with men within the framework of time and uses specific periods of time to accomplish

His purposes. What, then, is the relationship of these things to prophecy? We are quickly approaching the six thousandth year after Adam was created. Six is the number of man. One thousand years with man is as one day in God's eyes. We are, then, in the eleventh hour of man's sixth day. Since seven is God's number of perfection, it is not unreasonable to wonder if man's sixth day will end and God's day will begin at the end of this century.

At first glance, all these concepts may seem to be merely a numerical game. They could easily be dismissed as pure conjecture, except for three facts: (1) All of God's Word, even the numbers, is inspired by God. (2) The evidence, more of which we will present throughout this chapter, all adds up in exactly the way we might expect. (3) The numerical evidence, which is only a small percentage of the evidence, is confirmed by many other biblical signs.

What is the importance of the number four? Why should the fullness of time be four days, or 4,000 years, after the creation of man? The answer is simple and exciting. Biblical scholars are in agreement that Israel was cut off, at least temporarily, when the people rejected Jesus as the Messiah. This was prophesied in the Old Testament, as Peter and John preached after Pentecost.

The prophets also wrote that after the Messiah was rejected, Israel would be scattered among the nations. Keeping in mind that A.D. 2000 will mark the six thousandth anniversary of Adam's creation, and that a thousand years is as one day with God, consider the prophecy of Hosea concerning Israel's re-

A Prophetic Calendar

turn in the last days: "Come, and let us return unto the Lord: for he hath torn, and he will heal us; he hath smitten, and he will bind us up. After *two days* will he revive us: in the third day he will raise us up, and we shall live in his sight" (Hosea 6:1,2, italics mine).

Again, the biblical numbers speak for themselves. Israel was cut off after four days (4,000 years). She will be revived after two days. In the third day after her dispersion (the seventh day after the creation of man), Israel will live in God's sight in a new kingdom.

Another item of evidence substantiating this concept is associated with the Sabbath. There is no biblical evidence that any Gentile, except for Jewish proselytes, was ever commanded to keep the Sabbath. According to Exodus 31:12,13, the Sabbath was given to the Jews as a sign. It is not a matter of Christian command, but of Jewish promise.

It is a sign, but a sign of what? God rested on the seventh day of the week, after His creative will for Earth had been accomplished. Likewise, Israel was to rest on the Sabbath. A thousand years being as one day with God indicates that the Kingdom Age, when Christ reigns on earth as King of Kings, will begin with the seventh thousand-year period from Adam, foreshadowed when God rested on the seventh day. The seventh thousand-year day will begin in A.D. 2001, taking into account the four-year calendar error. This is why the Sabbath was a sign to Israel.

We are not the first to suggest that Christ might return by A.D. 2000. The deaths of Pope Paul VI and Pope John Paul I have caused many prognosticators to dig into the works and writings of some of the better-known seers and stargazers down through the centuries. We refer to the better-known ones in the sense that they had the greatest percentage of accurate predictions. We should keep in mind that only a prophet who can claim one hundred percent accuracy can claim inspiration from God. The only such prophets are the ones whose projections are recorded in the pages of the Bible under the affirmation of "Thus saith the Lord."

In any event, it appears that both Nostradamus of the sixteenth century and St. Malachy of the twelfth century made some rather astounding predictions. Both said that in the years before the end of this age a pope would reign for fifteen years. According to Nostradamus, his reign would be followed by a pope who would reign for thirty-four days. One interpreter infers that Malachy fixed the reign of this same pope at only twenty-eight days. Pope Paul VI reigned fifteen years. From the time of John Paul I's election to his death was thirty-four days. From the time of his coronation to his death was twenty-eight days.

The pope whose reign would be cut short was called the "barefoot pope." This could refer to the humble image projected by John Paul I.

According to Nostradamus, a French cardinal whose name would start with the letter "V" would become prominent during this time. After the death of the "barefoot pope," the projection says, another controversial pope would reign for a relatively short time. The next pope would then reign until the end of

A Prophetic Calendar

the world. It seems more than coincidental that Pope John Paul II has selected French Cardinal Jean Villot as his primary administrator over the Curia.

We in no way suggest that the writings of Nostradamus and Malachy be added to the canon, but it is interesting to observe that throughout the years men have, from some source or another, been making astounding predictions about these very days.

All these ancient prophecies came to light through a rather unusual source—an Associated Press release from Vatican City dated October 2, 1978. In the same article we find the interesting statement: "Nostradamus predicted events that will supposedly lead up to the end of the world in the year 2000. He mentioned in 'The Prophecies of Pope John' a 'barefoot pope' whose reign would last no more than two months and who would be succeeded by the last two popes."

From the fascinating study of biblical numerology, we have seen that Jesus Christ could come to establish His kingdom by the year 2000. Even some extra-biblical—and admittedly questionable—sources seem to point in that direction. The Old Testament, however, gives a very clear and distinct prophecy of the last times through Ezekiel. In Ezekiel 4 we read of the prophet's great concern—the redemption of Israel and the beginning of the Kingdom Age.

This concern covered several areas: (1) When would Jerusalem no longer be occupied by the enemy? (2) When would the people of Israel finally return home for good? (3) When would the people's sins be taken away so that the Lord could dwell in their midst?

God responded with a sign. He told Ezekiel to set a tile on the ground before him. The tile was to represent Jerusalem. He was told to lie on his left side before the tile for 390 days. He was then to lie on his right side for 40 days, making a total of 430 days. God told Ezekiel that each day he lay on his side was to represent one year.

In fulfillment of God's promise to Jeremiah, Israel remained in captivity in Babylon for 70 years. By subtracting those 70 years from Ezekiel's total of 430, we find 360 years for the fulfillment of the prophecy. However, even after they returned from Babylon, the people of Israel did not show true repentance. God had warned them in Leviticus 26:27,28: "If ye will not yet for all this hearken unto me . . . I will chastise you seven times for your sins."

Israel's complete deliverance was scheduled for 360 years after their return from Babylon, but because of their sin God multiplied their punishment seven times. Seven times 360 is 2,520 years.

Daniel's prophecy dovetails beautifully with Ezekiel's. Daniel said that 483 years would pass from the decree to rebuild the city of Jerusalem to the coming of the Messiah (Dan. 9:25,26). When we combine the 70 years of captivity, the 483 years from the end of the captivity to the coming of Jesus Christ, and the 1,967 years from the birth of Christ to the deliverance of Jerusalem from Gentile control during the war of 1967, we arrive at Ezekiel's number of

A Prophetic Calendar

2,520. The Israeli occupation of Jerusalem in the Six-Day War was no accident. Gentile control over Jerusalem ended exactly according to God's timetable.

Ezekiel's number has another significance. The prophet was also concerned with the Jews' permanent return to Palestine and the removal of their sins according to God's covenants with Abraham and David. According to Ussher's chronology,* the first contingent of Jews to return to Jerusalem arrived under the leadership of Zechariah and Haggai in 520 B.C. Counting forward 2,520 years from that date, we come to the year 2000. The promise that iniquity would be taken away is repeated in Romans 11:26,27: "And so all Israel shall be saved: as it is written, There shall come out of Sion the Deliverer, and shall turn away ungodliness from Jacob: For this is my covenant unto them, when I shall take away their sins."

Concerning the judgment predicted for the generation of Jesus' day, including the destruction of Jerusalem and the temple, Jesus said, "Verily I say unto you, All these things shall come upon this generation" (Matt. 23:36). He was speaking to adults, and in A.D. 70 the prophecy was fulfilled. The Scripture lists man's life span as seventy years. We believe that "a generation," as used in prophecy, is the full expected life span—the time it takes for one generation to appear and then pass away. When speaking of the generation who would see the beginning of the

*James Ussher (1581-1656) was an Irish prelate and scholar who worked out a series of dates setting creation at 4004 B.C.

signs of His second coming, Jesus said, "Verily, I say unto you, This generation shall not pass away, till all be fulfilled" (Luke 21:32).

Under the Old Testament system, God dealt with Israel in definite periods of years. Each period had a different significance. We see no reason why that pattern should not also point to the return of Christ. Consider the following:

Thirty is the Jewish age of maturity. No Jew could become a priest or hold political office until he was thirty. Jesus was thirty when He began His earthly ministry.

Forty is the number of testing. Israel was in the wilderness forty years. Jesus was in the wilderness forty days when he fasted and was tempted by Satan.

Fifty is the number of restoration, or jubilee. Every fiftieth year, the "year of jubilee," land was to be restored to its original owner.

Seventy years is the time of a complete generation. We read in Jeremiah 7:29 that God rejected the generation of Jeremiah's day. It then went into captivity for seventy years.

Prophetic analysts agree that the return of the Jews to Palestine is the most important event pointing to the return of Jesus. That return was made possible in 1917 by the signing of the Balfour Declaration. Jesus said that the same generation that saw the

A Prophetic Calendar

beginning of these prophetic signs would also see the completion of those signs.

The Balfour Declaration recognized the right of the Jews to return to Palestine and buy property there. We believe that this declaration is the budding of the fig tree—the first sign of Israel's revival. Assuming that 1917 is the starting date for the last generation and God's resumption of His dealing with Israel on a covenant basis, let us observe how important events in Israel have occurred in regular time periods, just as they did in Old Testament times.

First, thirty is the Jewish age of maturity. Thirty years after the Balfour Declaration was signed the Jews began to return to Palestine in significant numbers. Israel became powerful enough to be considered a sovereign nation. Her maturity as a new nation was proven when the small Israeli army defeated the combined forces of the Arab world.

Second, fifty is the Jewish number of restoration. Fifty years after the Balfour Declaration was signed—1967—Jerusalem was restored to Jewish control.

Third, seventy is the Jewish age for the life of one generation. Jesus said that the generation He was speaking to would see the destruction of Jerusalem. It did. He also said that the generation that saw the beginning of the great prophetic signs would also see His literal return. The seventieth year after the signing of the Balfour Declaration is 1987. This could be a very important year on God's prophetic calendar.

Fourth, forty is the Jewish number for testing. Since Israel was refounded as a nation in 1948, she has been tested like no other nation has been tested before. The will of the people to survive, to fight, and to sacrifice to keep their land against overwhelming odds is unparalleled in history. The Bible indicates that Israel will be tested until the Messiah comes. Forty years from 1948 is 1988. That also may be a very important year.

After the 1967 war, C. E. McLain wrote a prophetic study entitled *The Time of Christ's Coming*. In this booklet he suggested a timetable for the rebuilding of the temple in Jerusalem. Not only has God dealt with Israel in periods of thirty, forty, fifty, and seventy years, but He has also dealt with them in intervals of seven years. The ancient temple of Solomon was under construction for seven years. Jacob worked to gain his two wives in periods of seven years. The Tribulation period will be seven years long.

McLain concluded that after the Jews reclaimed the temple site in 1967, the temple could possibly be rebuilt seven years later—1974. The temple was not rebuilt by 1974, but in that year plans were announced and the foundation was laid for the Great Synagogue. As was stated in Chapter 1, the Great Synagogue will contain all the furnishings of the temple and could serve as the temple during the Tribulation.

A historical item in *Halley's Bible Handbook* states that when the Jews returned to rebuild the temple after the Babylonian captivity, 120 elders were ordained to reinstitute the Levitical order and sacrificial worship. This religious council that officiated from a central synagogue served as a temple until Zerubbabel's Temple could be completed. It was called the Great Synagogue. It seems evident that the second Great Synagogue could serve the same purpose.

If the Great Synagogue is to become the Tribulation temple, then we would expect its construction to be completed over a period of seven years. The foundation was begun in 1974. When we were at the site in March of 1978, workmen were busily pouring concrete and placing steel beams for the walls. We were told by Maurice Jaffee, who is in charge of the project, that it will probably be completed in 1981, taking a full seven years for its completion.

(Jaffe, executive vice president of Hechal Shlomo and president of the Union of Israel Synagogues, was kind enough to grant us extensive interviews in 1977 and again in March of 1979. He is looking for the soon coming of the Messiah as the hope of Israel. We tried to convince him that Jesus is the Messiah he is looking for, and he replied with a twinkle in his eye, "We'll just have to wait and see.")

Seven years after the completion of the Great Synagogue brings us again to the year 1988. Could it be that those seven years from 1981 to 1988 will be the Tribulation period? If so, then the Time of Jacob's Trouble, the final three and one-half years of the Tribulation when the worst of God's terrible judgments will be poured out, would correspond exactly to the final three and one-half years of Israel's forty-year testing period.

The Tribulation will end at Armageddon with the

return of Jesus Christ and the armies of heaven. The prophet Zechariah said that when He comes He will build a temple where representatives of all the nations will come to worship Him and learn His laws. This millennial temple is separate and distinct from the Tribulation temple. In all probability, this great temple will be constructed on the site of Solomon's grand original. The millennial temple is fully described in Ezekiel 40–48. If, like its predecessors, it takes seven years to complete, this new temple would be ready for occupancy in 1995. Of course, the year could actually be 1999 allowing for a possible calendar error of four years.

Will Jesus Christ be reigning on earth from His millennial temple by 2001? The internal evidence of Scripture indicates that He could be.

Let the reader understand that we in no way state without qualification that the Tribulation period will begin in 1981, that Jesus Christ will return in 1988, or that the millennial kingdom will be established by 2001. Only the brash or foolish would present such a dogmatic calendar for the Lord's return and the end-time events related to His coming.

However, we should keep in mind that Daniel knew from God's revelation to Jeremiah when the Babylonian captivity would end. If the religious leaders in Israel had rightfully understood the prophecy of Daniel's seventy weeks, they could have known when the Messiah would be born, and even when He would be crucified.

The calculations and timetables set forth in this chapter are to be considered only as further evidence that God's timepiece for this present age is rapidly ticking off the remaining seconds. As God's watchmen in this generation, it is our responsibility to present all the signs that are in evidence so that no one is ignorant of the times in which we live (2 Pet. 3:5,8).

THREE

The Budding Fig Tree

> Now learn a parable of the fig tree; When his branch is yet tender, and putteth forth leaves, ye know that summer is nigh: So likewise ye, when ye shall see all these things, know that it is near, even at the doors. Verily I say unto you, This generation shall not pass, till all these things be fulfilled (Matt. 24:32-34).

Jesus made it very clear that the generation that witnessed the beginning of His prophetic signs—the budding of the fig tree—would be the same generation that would witness His visible return. Throughout the Old Testament it is impossible to separate the promises of Christ's coming from the regathering of Israel. The coming together of Israel as a nation under the reign of the Son of David is the central theme of all Old Testament prophecy. Jesus' own projections of the events surrounding His return are linked inexorably to the Jewish possession of Palestine and Jerusalem.

Israel, now returned to the land from which she has been scattered for hundreds of years, is the most

The Budding Fig Tree

important sign we have of the last days. Let us closely examine some of the prophecies related to this chosen nation.

As we have already noted, the return of Israel to Palestine was made possible by the signing of the Balfour Declaration in 1917. If that year marked the beginning of the prophetic signs of the end times, then the following years should have contained an increasing number of signs. They have.

Israel has always been a miracle nation. As long as she was faithful to God, He poured out His blessings. According to Zechariah 12:6, God will watch over this tiny nation in the last days.

> In that day will I make the governors of Judah like an hearth of fire among the wood, and like a torch of fire in a sheaf; and they shall devour all the people round about, on the right hand and on the left: and Jerusalem shall be inhabited again in her own place, even in Jerusalem.

This prophecy was fulfilled in 1967 when the Israeli army defeated the nations to its right—Syria and Jordan—and to its left—Egypt. The military victory was nothing short of miraculous, but it wasn't the first time Israel had experienced such a modern-day deliverance.

Twenty years before the Six-Day War, the growing number of Jews in Palestine were preparing to declare themselves an independent Jewish state. The year was 1947, and U.S. General George Marshall had a stern warning for Jewish leader David Ben Gurion. "For God's sake," Marshall warned, "tell your people in Palestine they shouldn't proclaim a Jewish state. If they proclaim a Jewish state, within ten days or a maximum of fifteen days not a single Jew will remain alive."*

Marshall was a five-star general, the highest-ranking officer of the mightiest military power in the world at the time. He should have known what he was talking about. He knew military strategy, but he did not know that God had determined the outcome of this particular war 2,400 years earlier.

When the sovereignty of Israel was proclaimed on May 14, 1948, the combined armies of Egypt, Jordan, Syria, Lebanon, Iraq, and Saudi Arabia attacked an Israeli army of raw recruits who were outnumbered thirty to one. Marshall never had the opportunity to deliver his "I-told-you-so" speech. When the smoke cleared, Israel had won.

Such a victory is beyond human reasoning, but not beyond divine provision. According to human reasoning, Sarah should not have given birth to Isaac. According to human reasoning, David didn't stand a chance against Goliath. And according to human reasoning, Israel should long ago have been pushed into the Mediterranean Sea. Yet she won miracle victories in 1948, 1967, and 1973.

It is a miracle that the Jewish people have survived as a race after being scattered among the nations of the world for almost 2,000 years. It is a miracle that they have returned to the land. It is a

*H. S. DeWeerd, ed., *Selected Speeches & Statements of General of the Army George C. Marshall* (New York: DaCapo Press, 1973).

miracle that as soon as their feet touched the ground on which Abraham trod they became a social, political, and military entity. According to the prophecies of God, they have stumbled back into the land—still blinded to the Light of the world, still in unbelief. Nevertheless, the sign is unmistakable. The fig tree has budded. Israel has returned to her promised land.

In looking forward to Israel's dispersion among the nations, Hosea wrote: "For the children of Israel shall abide many days without a king, and without a prince, and without a sacrifice, and without an image, and without an ephod, and without teraphim" (Hos. 3:4). The fulfillment of that prophecy is history.

In looking forward to the time following the dispersion, Hosea continued: "Afterward shall the children of Israel return, and seek the Lord their God, and David their king; and shall fear the Lord and his goodness in the latter days" (Hos. 3:5).

The return of Israel to the land is prophesied over and over again in the Old Testament. Isaiah wrote: "Fear not: for I am with thee: I will bring thy seed from the east, and gather thee from the west; I will say to the north, Give up; and to the south, Keep not back: bring my sons from far, and my daughters from the ends of the earth" (Isa. 43:5,6).

During the years of the dispersion many theologians spiritualized the promises and covenants to Israel, imagining that in some way these promises were fulfilled in the church. Prophecies relating to the refounding of Israel as a nation were interpreted as referring to a kingdom brought about on earth through the efforts of the church. Even today, the Catholic church has not recognized the rights of the Jews to possess the old city of Jerusalem.

In a day when a literal return to the land of Palestine by the Jews seemed very unlikely, there were courageous ministers who steadfastly claimed that the promises given to Israel would be fulfilled in Israel. History has vindicated them. In 1863, John Owen said, "The Jews shall be gathered from all parts of the earth where they are now scattered, and brought back into their own land. . . . The Lord Christ himself being their king, who shall then also be acknowledged King over all the earth."

In 1864, Charles Spurgeon wrote, "Israel is now blotted out from the map of nations: her sons are scattered far and wide; her daughters mourn beside the rivers of the earth. . . . But she is to be restored. . . . There will be a native government again; there will again be the form of a body politic."

Jews have returned to Israel from almost every nation in the world. Most countries have allowed them to return willingly; some, like the Arab nations, were actually glad to be rid of them. Russia demands that all Jews pay a ransom before leaving. The Jews in Israel are but a remnant, accounting for less than one fourth of the total Jewish population. They still have not recognized Jesus as Messiah, but in spite of their unbelief their very presence in Palestine is the single most important sign that Jesus will return to earth soon.

There are other ramifications of Israel's presence in Palestine. God gave the land to the seed of

Abraham through Isaac. When the seed of Abraham through Isaac and Jacob are in possession of the land, it prospers. When they are absent from the land, it withers and is only good for keeping goats. This happened during the Babylonian captivity and again during the dispersion.

Only when Jews began returning to the land in great numbers following World War II did the land begin to blossom again with fruit and vegetation. True, a great deal of hard work went into the renovation of the countryside, but it is according to God's will and prophetic Word. Only when the Jews possess the land does it prosper and blossom like a rose (Isa. 35:1).

As interesting as the concept of Israel's return may be, we should not overlook the prophetic importance of the manner in which the Jews have returned. As we have already noted, the Balfour Declaration granted Jews the right to return to Palestine and *buy* land there from Arab owners. This was not to be a military conquest. Thus, the territory that comprised the newly founded nation of Israel consisted largely of land that the Jews had purchased. Consider the words of Jeremiah on this very subject:

> For thus saith the Lord; Like as I have brought all this great evil upon this people, so will I bring upon them all the good that I have promised them. And fields shall be bought in this land, whereof ye say, It is desolate without man or beast; it is given into the hand of the Chaldeans. Men shall buy fields for money, and subscribe evidences, and seal them,

and take witnesses in the land of Benjamin, and in the places about Jerusalem, and in the cities of Judah, and in the cities of the mountains, and in the cities of the valley, and in the cities of the south: for I will cause their captivity to return, saith the Lord (Jer. 32:42–44).

The February 28, 1977, issue of *Time* magazine reported that Israel has developed a large section of the Sinai area from the Mediterranean Sea to the Gulf of Suez. Roads, cities, and schools have been built. Water lines have been laid in the desert. In Isaiah 19:18 we are told of such changes that would be made by Israel during the last days: "In that day shall five cities in the land of Egypt speak the language of Canaan, and swear to the Lord of hosts; one shall be called, The city of destruction."

In the Six-Day War of June, 1967, Israel captured all of the Sinai peninsula. Within this area there are five major cities. Hebrew, the official language of the land of Canaan today, was taught in the schools in these cities during the time of the Israeli occupation. According to the prophecy, one of the cities would be called "the city of destruction." The city of El Arish on the Mediterranean Sea was among the cities occupied by Israel. Its name literally means "the city of destruction."

In another prophecy Ezekiel wrote, "And I will pour my fury upon Sin, the strength of Egypt; and I will cut off the multitude of No. And I will set fire in Egypt: Sin shall have great pain, and No shall be rent asunder, and Noph shall have distresses daily. . . .

The Budding Fig Tree

and they shall know that I am the Lord" (Ezek. 30:15,16,19).

"No" was an area of canal systems in Egypt, eventually replaced by the Suez Canal. "Sin" is easily identified as the area east of Suez; it is the root name from which the entire Sinai region is named. "Noph" is the capital of lower Egypt and the ancient name for the modern city of Cairo. As Ezekiel prophesied, the multitude of ships was cut off from "No." Only in 1976 was the Suez Canal reopened for traffic. God's fury was poured out on "Sin" in both 1967 and 1973, and as the prophet foretold, there was great distress in Cairo during those days.

Political and geographical changes are occurring rapidly throughout the Middle East, and such changes are both interesting and exciting to the student of prophecy. Watching the events unfold is similar to viewing a play after having read a synopsis of the drama. We recognize the main characters and we are able to forecast many of the major twists in the plot. We are certain, in advance, of exactly how the story will end.

In watching the Middle East, we only have to consult Scripture to identify the main characters. The climax of the drama will be the glorious return of Jesus Christ. We have no way of knowing how extensively or how often territory will change hands in the Sinai. The historic peace talks at Camp David and the subsequent signing of a peace treaty between Israel and Egypt have added a fascinating twist to the plot.

None of the prophecies of the last days could be meaningful until Palestine and Jerusalem were again in the hands of the Jews. Each new development in Middle East politics only serves to underline the fact that we are rushing toward the finale, the climax, the conclusion of this part of history. Jesus is coming back; and it is exciting to think that many of this generation will live to see His coming in the clouds.

FOUR
Elijah Must Come

The Old Testament ends with the prophecy to Israel: "Behold, I will send you Elijah the prophet before the coming of the great and dreadful day of the Lord: And he shall turn the heart of the fathers to the children, and the heart of the children to their fathers, lest I come and smite the earth with a curse" (Mal. 4:5,6). That Elijah will appear on this earth as a witness to Israel before the coming of Israel's Messiah is beyond question. What we want to discuss now is why the prophet must come and what he will do.

The name Elijah means "God is Jehovah." The emphasis of his message was "If the Lord be God, follow him: but if Baal, then follow him" (1 Kings 18:21). The highlights of his life and mission are recorded in 1 Kings 17–19 and 2 Kings 2 as follows:

He was a rough mountain man called by God to restore faith in the Lord in Israel.
He predicted a drought in the northern kingdom.
He was fed by a raven, a widow, and an angel.

He raised the widow's son from death.

He defeated the prophets of Baal and had them slain.

He confronted King Ahab with his sins and apostasy.

He restored the animal sacrifice commanded by the law.

He was chased out of the nation by Ahab's wicked wife, Jezebel.

He returned and brought about the demise of the idolatrous queen.

He brought justice to the poor and lowly.

He was taken up into heaven in a whirling chariot of fire.

Because of the ministry of Elijah, the northern kingdom was preserved for seventy years. Although there was no permanent and lasting revival in Israel, and even Ahab returned to his evil doings, for the sake of Elijah's disciple Elisha and the faith of those strengthened by the prophet the nation was spared from God's judgment for a time. The ministry of Elijah during the reign of Ahab and Jezebel gives us a clue as to his mission when he will appear in Israel again during the reign of Antichrist and the religious system called Jezebel, the wicked harlot of the Tribulation period.

The biblical account of the catching up of Elijah into heaven in a vehicle of God is accepted as fact in Jewish history. Josephus wrote of this miracle:

> Now at this time it was that Elijah disappeared from among men, and no one knows of his death to this

Elijah Must Come

very day; but he left behind him his disciple Elisha, as we have formerly declared. And indeed, as to Elijah, and as to Enoch, who was before the Deluge, it is written in the sacred books that they disappeared; but so that nobody knew that they died (Josephus, Antiquities of the Jews, Book IX, Chapter II).

Enoch was translated so that he might not see death (Heb. 11:5), and it appears evident from Scripture that Elijah was likewise translated.

Elijah and John the Baptist

There is much confusion among theologians concerning the connection between the ministry of Elijah and that of John the Baptist. Malachi prophesied:

Behold, I will send my messenger, and he shall prepare the way before me: and the Lord, whom ye seek, shall suddenly come to his temple, even the messenger of the covenant, whom ye delight in: behold, he shall come, saith the Lord of hosts. But who may abide the day of his coming? and who shall stand when he appeareth? for he is like a refiner's fire, and like fullers' soap (Mal. 3:1,2).

This prophecy looked forward to John the Baptist, but John did not fulfill all the prophecy. It can only be completed when Christ returns. John the Baptist did come in the spirit of Elijah. They were of the same nature and spirit, and were similar in speech, dress, and diet. John came to prepare the way for the Lord, for when Jesus appeared on the scene John immediately proclaimed: "Behold the Lamb of God, which taketh away the sin of the world" (John 1:29).

In the spirit of Elijah, John the Baptist confronted evil King Herod and his adulterous wife Herodias with their sins. Indeed, many believed that John was Elijah returned from heaven. Most New Testament commentaries affirm that John the Baptist fulfilled the Old Testament prophecy that Elijah would come before the day of the Lord. Matthew Henry's commentary states rather boldly: ". . . we Christians know very well that John the Baptist was the Elijah that was to come." It is difficult for us to agree with such a positive statement. We believe that the Scriptures, on careful examination, clearly teach otherwise.

In Matthew 11:10,13–15, Jesus declared of John:

> For this is he, of whom it is written, Behold, I send my messenger before thy face, which shall prepare thy way before thee. . . . For all the prophets and the law prophesied until John. And if ye will receive it, this is Elias, which was for to come. He that hath ears to hear, let him hear.

The message and prophecy of the writings of the law and the prophets covered all that Israel needed to know from God until the appearance of John the Baptist. John came with an additional message, which in essence was, "Repent, for the kingdom of heaven is at hand. The King is here—make yourselves ready for His kingdom."

Jesus told His disciples that if Israel believed and accepted John's message and received Jesus Christ as Lord and King, then John would have indeed fulfilled the prophecy about Elijah as coming first and restoring all things. But Jesus knew that the message of John would be rejected, and that the real Elijah must come at some time in the future.

This truth is set forth in Matthew 17:10-13:

> And his disciples asked him, saying, Why then say the scribes that Elias must first come? And Jesus answered and said unto them, Elias truly shall first come, and restore all things. But I say unto you, That Elias is come already, and they knew him not, but have done unto him whatsoever they listed. Likewise shall also the Son of man suffer of them. Then the disciples understood that he spake unto them of John the Baptist.

John did not restore all things; neither did he bring repentance to Israel nor make the way ready for Jesus to reign on David's throne. Therefore, Jesus said that because John was rejected He must suffer—meaning that He would go to the cross and that the same Elijah who stood before Ahab would return to the earth and bring to pass all that was prophesied.

Books of the Bible—The Twelve Prophets is a commentary on the Hebrew text of the Old Testament that offers the consensus of the best Jewish scholarship of all time on the law and the prophets. The following presents the traditional Jewish beliefs about the coming of Elijah:

> Elijah the prophet . . . the messenger who will prepare the way for the coming of the Lord . . . is to later generations the helper and healer, the reconciler and peace-bringer, the herald of the days of the Messiah. . . . Unless Elijah succeeds in his task, ruin faces the Land of Israel. . . . Elijah's mission is to bring peace to the world . . . [and] herald the advent of the Messiah, and turn mankind to their Father in heaven.*

The "Feast of the Passover," observed in Jewish homes during Passover week, begins on the fifteenth of the Jewish month Nisan and has always pointed forward to the Messiah. But Paul wrote that Jesus Christ is our Passover and was sacrificed for us (1 Cor. 5:7). At every Passover meal in Jewish homes there is an empty chair at the table. This chair is for the prophet Elijah, who must come to prepare the way for the Messiah.

When Is Elijah Coming?

We come now to the question: When is Elijah coming? The prophet Malachi placed the coming of Elijah some time before "the coming of the great and dreadful day of the Lord." J. Dwight Pentecost, in his book *Things To Come*, presents a host of opinions by theologians concerning the time element of the "day of the Lord." It seems to us that the "day of the Lord" can extend from the beginning of the Tribulation to the end of the Kingdom Age.

---

*Dr. A. Cohen, ed., *Books of the Bible—The Twelve Prophets* (London: Soncino Press, 1948), p. 356.

We must not be too dogmatic about how long Elijah will be on the earth before Christ returns. Nowhere in the New Testament is the church admonished to look for the coming of Elijah; therefore we conclude that the prophet will begin his ministry after all Christians are taken out of the world.

For purposes of this study, we will say that Elijah probably will come at least seven years prior to the literal return of the Lord, and possibly even earlier, although we doubt seriously that he will return much before the Tribulation. If Elijah were to come before the rapture of the church, his mission would conflict with our Christian mission to win both Jew and Gentile to Christ, making one body of both. Obviously, Elijah would not return until Israel had been refounded as a nation. If Elijah is in the world today, it is unlikely that he can or will begin his ministry to Israel until after the church is raptured.

Why Is Elijah Coming?

In considering why Elijah must come back, we need look no further than Malachi 4:5,6: "Behold, I will send you Elijah the prophet before the coming of the great and dreadful day of the Lord . . . lest I come and smite the earth with a curse." God cursed the ground after Adam and Eve sinned, and the creation on earth was changed (Gen. 3:16–19). God cursed the ground again at the Flood, and the creation was changed again (Gen. 8:21,22). If Elijah did not come to prepare the remnant of Israel to accept Jesus Christ as Lord, Savior, and King of Kings, the earth would be cursed for a third time.

Notice the wording in Malachi 4:6: ". . . lest I come and smite the earth with a curse." Whether or not the Lord will come is not the question. Both Old and New Testament prophecy declares that Jesus Christ is coming back to the earth. The question presented by Malachi is, "Will the Lord curse the earth when He comes?"

The answer depends upon the ministry of Elijah. Of course, we know from prophecy that Jesus Christ will not have to curse the earth again. He will restore it to its condition and environment prior to the curse resulting from sin. It is made clear in Revelation 11:18 that Jesus will come back and save the earth, not curse or destroy it. Of course, after His millennial reign, the earth as we know it will be destroyed by fire (see 2 Pet. 3:7).

What Will Elijah Do?

The prophetic Word indicates that Elijah is going to be very busy when he comes. The first thing he will do is prophesied in Malachi 4:6: "And he shall turn the heart of the fathers to the children, and the heart of the children to their fathers." Of course, John the Baptist did fulfill this prophecy in a very small way.

The Hebrew commentary mentioned earlier interprets this promise thusly:

> He shall turn the heart of the fathers to the children. Family discord was the natural result of the divorces and foreign marriages which the prophet denounced, and family life was in danger of disinte-

gration. Elijah will restore harmony in the homes, and will turn the hearts of all to God.*

The Judaic concept of separation from the world and holiness before God had almost disappeared when Elijah appeared on the scene in Israel. Jezebel had brought in foreign and idolatrous men and women, and through Ahab's example of marrying a foreign and licentious woman, the northern kingdom was rapidly becoming a mixed nation both in race and religion. Elijah restored the concept of national and religious purity.

Today, Israel is much more liberal than orthodox. Elijah will again restore the Jewish family structure, both in morals and national identity. This was the commandment given to the prophet to prepare the people of Israel for the coming of the Lord, and it is a prerequisite for the coming of Christ to reign on David's throne over God's earthly and peculiar people.

Fight Against Jezebel

Elijah's mortal enemy was the wicked queen Jezebel, who forced Baal worship upon the nation. The fight between the prophet and the queen is fully recorded in the closing chapters of 1 Kings and the beginning chapters of 2 Kings. Jezebel was the power behind King Ahab.

Most Protestant scholars of prophecy interpret the Thyatiran church age of Revelation 2:18–23 as the world church that had power over the nations be-

*Cohen, ed., *Books of the Bible*, p. 356.

tween the years, 500 and 1500. We read of this Thyatiran religious system:

> ... I have a few things against thee, because thou sufferest that woman Jezebel, which calleth herself a prophetess, to teach and to seduce my servants to commit fornication, and to eat things sacrificed unto idols. And I gave her space to repent of her fornication; and she repented not. Behold, I will cast her into a bed, and them that commit adultery with her into great tribulation, except they repent of their deeds (Rev. 2:20–22).

The religious system identified as Jezebel continues into the Great Tribulation as prophesied, and we read of it in Revelation 17:4,5 as the woman ". . . arrayed in purple and scarlet colour, and decked with gold and precious stones and pearls, having a golden cup in her hand full of abominations and filthiness of her fornication: And upon her forehead was a name written, MYSTERY, BABYLON THE GREAT, THE MOTHER OF HARLOTS AND ABOMINATIONS OF THE EARTH."

This system will become the harlot church of the false messiah, the Antichrist. The False Prophet, identified as the ecclesiastical head of the harlot church, will command that every person on the face of the earth fall down and worship the image of the Antichrist and take his number and mark or be slain. There are interesting developments in religion today that foreshadow the fight between the Jezebel of Revelation and Elijah.

The social gospel has seduced the modernistic

churches of our day. This strange doctrine makes the mission of the church the distribution of property and the social and economic improvement of the human race. The World Council of Churches, in its 1966 Geneva Convention, outlined the mission of all affiliate churches as the promotion of political revolution in order to bring a more just political government to all nations. The new pope of the Catholic church, John Paul II, has determined to try to work out an accommodation with Communist governments. For the first time in history, Communist representatives attended the coronation of a pope.

All these events foreshadow a future union of the religious and political units of the whole economy of this world, as prophesied in Revelation 13. The one-world politically controlled church of the Great Tribulation will be the Great Whore, the power behind the world throne, just as Jezebel was the power behind King Ahab in the days of Elijah. God will again send Elijah to fight against Jezebel.

Elijah and the Two Witnesses

Some facets of orthodox Jewish theology indicate that both Moses and Elijah are to come back before the "great and terrible day of the Lord." Both Moses and Elijah appeared on the Mount of Transfiguration with Jesus—a preview of Christ coming into His kingdom on earth. Thus it is reasonable to say that Moses and Elijah will be the two witnesses of Revelation 11.

This is also indicated by their supernatural powers (Rev. 11:5). Just as it did not rain in Israel for three and one-half years during the first ministry of Elijah, it will not rain during the Tribulation for three and one-half years. The two witnesses will also have the power to bring plagues such as those that occurred in Egypt when Moses led God's people out of that land.

In any event, the Antichrist ultimately will be successful in killing the two witnesses, as recorded prophetically in Revelation 11:9: "And they of the people and kindreds and tongues and nations shall see their dead bodies three days and an half. . . ." This will be a simple matter via television. In fact, this prophecy could not have been fulfilled until an international television network became possible.

Elijah and Christ's Coming

The ministry of Elijah "before the great and dreadful day of the Lord" will be successful. He will turn the heart of every Jew left at that time to God. He will restore the race to a truly peculiar and separated position. When Jesus Christ appears to Israel the second time, they will believe on Him not only as Lord of Lords and King of Kings, but also as the Redeemer Who died for their sins: "And I will pour upon the house of David, and upon the inhabitants of Jerusalem, the spirit of grace and of supplications: and they shall look upon me whom they have pierced, and they shall mourn for him, as one mourneth for his only son . . ." (Zech. 12:10).

Then the prophecy of Romans 11:26, 27 will be fulfilled: "And so all Israel shall be saved: as it is written, There shall come out of Sion the Deliverer, and shall turn away ungodliness from Jacob [all twelve tribes]: For this is my covenant unto them, when I shall take away their sins."

FIVE

Nations in the Net

"So likewise ye, when ye shall see all these things, know that it is near, even at the doors" (Matt. 24:33).

Jesus said there would be certain signs that point to His return. The importance of His words in Matthew is that He appears to have divided these signs into two categories. First, certain prophetic events should alert us to the reality that His coming is near. Second, other events should tell us that His coming is at the door. We will refer to these as "near signs" and "at-the-door signs."

Near Signs

We have already discussed most of the near events. We will list them here only briefly.

The first sign is *the return of Israel to the land of Palestine*. This first alerted Christians that the return of Christ was near.

The second sign is *the refounding of Israel as a nation*. When the fig tree began blossoming (Matt. 24:32–36), Christians could be certain that the coming of Jesus was approaching.

The third near sign is *wars and rumors of wars*. War has always been with us, but the twentieth century has been the most war-prone period in human history. Half of all known war casualties have occurred in the past sixty years.

The fourth sign is *famine*. The World Health Organization projects that one billion people will die due to famine in the next ten years.

False prophets and false Christs are the fifth sign. An Associated Press release several years ago heralded the fact that gods are on the increase in the United States. The article noted that "Jesus predicted a rise of false 'Christs' and 'gods' as the world moved toward its consummation." This is certainly an interesting statement from a secular source.

The popularity of cults and false religions is increasing. Not only has interest increased in the traditional oriental religions, but newer cults such as the Unification Church of Sun Myung Moon are also on the rise. The horror of the Jonestown suicide/massacre serves only to underline the total mystical control such false religious movements can exercise over their victims.

The sixth sign is an *increase in knowledge*. About seventy percent of all young people receive a college education, when only about ten percent of all available jobs require college training. Education is almost universally touted as the answer to any and all of man's problems.

The *increase in travel* is the seventh sign. People travel more often and faster than at any time in history. Man is, as the prophet wrote, running to and fro on the face of the earth.

The eighth near sign is the *increase in occult activity*. Paul wrote in 1 Timothy 4:1 that in the latter days many people would be deceived by "seducing spirits." Never before in modern history has there been such an interest in astrology, witchcraft, demonism, and Satan worship.

The ninth sign is *the revival of ancient cities and nations* that were formerly desolate. The cities of Tyre and Sidon, once passed over by modern civilization, are frequently in the news. There is talk of rebuilding Babylon. Iran, the biblical Persia, is in the center of world attention. Jerusalem, Damascus, Libya, Ethiopia, and many other biblical sites are now making headlines in our daily newspapers (Isa. 58:12; 61:4).

Increasing lawlessness and moral decay is the tenth of these near signs (Matt. 24:37; 2 Tim. 3:1–7).

These are only a few of the many signs that tell us Christ's coming is near. There are others, but these are the most important.

At-The-Door Signs

We have seen all the previously mentioned signs fulfilled, either wholly or in part, during our lifetime. They constitute an irrefutable volume of truth, even to the secular world, that this age is nearing its end. Jesus said that certain signs would occur that, if carefully compared to Bible prophecy, would reveal that His return is not only near, but actually at the door. Some of the at-the-door signs are listed here.

The first is *the covenant between Israel and her enemies*. Daniel 9:27 reveals that a seven-year treaty will bring peace to the Middle East. In return for certain concessions, Israel will receive a guaranteed right to the land of Palestine. The period of this treaty is the Tribulation, at the end of which Jesus will return to establish His reign on earth. Exactly seven years after this treaty is signed, Jesus will return. Of course, the believers of the Church Age will not be present during the Tribulation, having been caught away probably just before the treaty is signed.

The second sign will be *the building of the Jewish temple*. The appearance of a Jewish temple in Jerusalem will allow the nation to resume religious services as outlined by the Mosaic law, including animal sacrifice. Like so many peace treaties, the covenant with Israel will be only a temporary arrangement to a political end. After three and one-half years, the treaty will be broken. Religious services in the temple will be stopped, and the Jews will have to flee for their lives. Exactly forty-two months after this happens, Jesus Christ will return. However, the temple must be rebuilt before any of these events can happen (Dan. 9:27; Matt. 24:15; Rev. 11,12,13).

The third at-the-door sign is *the alignment of all nations against Israel*. Armies from all nations will march against Israel at the end of the Great Tribulation (Zech. 14:1–7). Already, in 1967, the United Nations unanimously condemned Israel, with the United States abstaining. Only the return of Christ will spare Israel from total annihilation.

The fourth sign is *strange occurrences in the heavens*. Scripture tells us that the sun will become seven times hotter than normal, then become dark

(Isa. 30:26; Rev. 16:8,9; Joel 2:30,31; Matt. 24:29). All these prophecies of extraordinary solar activity indicate that it will take place only days before Christ's return.

The fifth sign, *earthquakes*, could be classified both as a near sign and an at-the-door sign. Jesus said in Matthew 24:7 that the increase of earthquakes, both in number and intensity, would be a sign of His return. However, during the Great Tribulation there will be three tremendously strong earthquakes. The final one will be so strong that it will level mountains and sink islands (Ezek. 38:20; Rev. 16:18).

The sixth sign is *the mark of the Beast*. Revelation 13:11–18 tells us that approximately three and one-half years before Christ's return a worldwide religious, political, and economic system will be forced on all nations. Everyone in the world will be ordered to serve and worship a man who will set himself up as a savior of the world. This man will claim to be the Messiah of Israel and the Savior of all mankind. Everyone who does not submit to him and receive his mark will be unable to work, buy, or operate a business. When this new, oppressive economic system is instituted, the return of Jesus will be three and one-half years away, or less.

There are some who say that no signs of the end of the age and the return of Jesus Christ are given to the church, and that the church could be raptured at any time. (As noted in Chapter 2, by "raptured" we mean that the Christians of the Church Age will be taken up from the earth to be with the Lord just prior to the Tribulation.)

We would dispute the claim that no signs are committed to the church. Paul wrote in his epistles that in the last days there would be apostasy in the church, increased lawlessness, and a breakdown of family relationships. It is true that the preponderance of signs points to the coming of Christ in glory, not to the Rapture. Still, the fulfillment of so many of these signs must surely indicate that the Church-Age believers will be leaving this earth very soon.

It is our conviction that no Christian living at the time of the Rapture will witness the complete fulfillment of any one of the at-the-door signs. Nevertheless, even now the shadows of these signs are being cast upon the doorsteps. Efforts to negotiate peace in the Middle East are continuing. Could the Antichrist's covenant be far in the future? The Great Synagogue, a modern-day replica of the Jewish temple, is already under construction and should be completed in 1981. The nations of the world are aligning themselves against Israel. Earthquakes are occurring with unprecedented intensity and frequency. Modern computer systems have made the numbering and electronic control of the world economy a present-day possibility—just the tool the Antichrist will require to maintain his stranglehold on the world.

We have, however, purposely passed over one of the most significant and amazing at-the-door signs—what we believe is Christ's prediction of the exact number of nations that will exist in the world at the time of His return.

Nations In the Net

The seventh prophecy that may be classified as an at-the-door sign deals with nets. At least sixteen times in prophecy, the establishment of Christ's kingdom is referred to symbolically as a fisherman drawing in his net. In speaking to the rebellious nation of Egypt, God said, "I will therefore spread out my net over thee with a company of many people; and they shall bring thee up in my net" (Ezek. 32:3).

Cruden's Concordance gives the following definition for the word "net" in Scripture: "A woven fabric for catching fish or birds; hence a snare, trap. It is also used figuratively, as for difficulties in which one is caught; or the trap set by one's enemies."

Chapters 12–14 of the prophecy of Zechariah outline a trap, a snare, a net that the Lord will set for the nations of the world. He will lure them in hatred to Jerusalem, but as they besiege the city He will destroy them. We see the beginning of this gathering already.

But does the Bible tell us how many nations will be caught in this trap God is preparing? We believe it does. We believe that 153 armies will be massed against Israel at Armageddon. We see this as a prophetic interpretation of John 21.

The chapter begins with the account of the disciples attempting to catch fish in the Sea of Tiberias, the name the Romans gave to the Sea of Galilee. The fact that the Gentile name for Galilee is used should alert us that this particular episode has a Gentile application. The disciples had been fishing all night and had not caught a single fish.

Beginning in verse 4, we read:

> But when the morning was now come, Jesus stood on the shore: but the disciples knew not that it was Jesus. Then Jesus saith unto them, Children, have ye any meat? They answered him, No. And he said unto them, Cast the net on the right side of the ship, and ye shall find. They cast therefore, and now they were not able to draw it for the multitude of fishes. Therefore that disciple whom Jesus loved saith unto Peter, It is the Lord. Now when Simon Peter heard that it was the Lord, he girt his fisher's coat unto him, (for he was naked,) and did cast himself into the sea. And the other disciples came in a little ship; (for they were not far from land, but as it were two hundred cubits,) dragging the net with fishes. As soon then as they were come to land, they saw a fire of coals there, and fish laid thereon, and bread. Jesus saith unto them, Bring of the fish which ye have now caught. Simon Peter went up, and drew the net to land full of great fishes, an hundred and fifty and three: and for all there were so many, yet was not the net broken (John 21:4–11).

Regardless of whether the account of the net and fishes is interpreted as illustrating soul-winning or the return of Christ, there is much agreement that the teaching is presented in symbolic language. We make the application to Christ's literal return at the end of the Great Tribulation for several reasons.

First the disciples had been fishing all night. The

night is often used in prophetic symbolism to represent the Tribulation period.

> For yourselves know perfectly that the day of the Lord so cometh as a thief in the night. For when they shall say, Peace and safety; then sudden destruction cometh upon them, as travail upon a woman with child; and they shall not escape (1 Thess. 5:2,3).

Second, the disciples who followed Jesus' instructions in casting forth their net were apostles. The twelve apostles will be with the Lord when He brings in the kingdom.

> Then answered Peter and said unto him, Behold, we have forsaken all, and followed thee; what shall we have therefore? And Jesus said unto them, Verily I say unto you, That ye which have followed me, in the regeneration when the Son of man shall sit in the throne of his glory, ye also shall sit upon twelve thrones, judging the twelve tribes of Israel (Matt. 19:27,28).

Third, the apostle Peter led the procession as the net brought the fish to shore. Peter is the kingdom apostle. Jesus committed to Peter the keys of the kingdom (Matt. 16:19).

Fourth, the net was dragged 200 cubits to land, a normal distance to drag a net full of fish. If the net had been dragged 2 cubits, 20 cubits, or 2,000 cubits, it would have been an abnormal distance, and thus the teaching would have been cast in unrealistic sym-

Nations in the Net

bolism. It is our contention that all numbers in Scripture are important. Since we consider this account to be representative teaching, we must consider what the 200 cubits represent.

For comparative purposes, consider God's number of testing—40. We have already seen how God tested Israel over time periods of 40, both days and years. In His grace and wisdom, God has occasionally multiplied the time of testing by His number of completion—10. For example, the Israelites were in Egypt for 400 years. They were under the judges for 400 years. Judah was under kings for 400 years and without a prophet for 400 years (from Malachi to the birth of Christ).

Applying the same principle of multiplication to this passage, we have the figure 2,000. We have already seen that the 2 days Hosea prophesied for Israel's dispersion may represent 2,000 years. The concept of 1,000-year days, divided into 6 days of man and 1 day of the Lord, point to a period of 2,000 years from the earthly ministry of Christ until His glorious return. The prophecies of both Ezekiel and Daniel (as presented in Chapter 2) point to the establishment of Christ's earthly kingdom near A.D. 2000.

This, we believe, is the true significance of the 200 cubits. They picture the 2,000 years of the dispensation of grace—that period of time between Christ's first and second advent.

Fifth, the fact that there were exactly 153 fish mentioned must indicate a teaching broader in scope than merely a challenge to soul-winning. Christian converts are numbered only in the first few chapters of Acts, and then only incidentally. Nowhere in the gospel of grace, given to Paul for presentation to the Gentiles, were Christians numbered. If the exact number of fish is not important, then why is the exact number recorded? We believe it is only reasonable to conclude, in light of the evident Kingdom Age teaching, that the 153 fish represent the nations Jesus will catch in His net when He comes back.

As far as we know, we were the first to present this explanation of the number of fish in John 21. We suggested in 1970 that they represent the nations at the second advent of Christ—when there were still only 139 nations. We understand that now this explanation is being introduced in eschatology studies in some seminaries. (One of the most noted is Moody Bible Institute.)

The 1979 edition of *Award World Atlas* by Hammond lists the present membership of the United Nations at 154 nations, one more than the prophetic implication this particular interpretation might suggest.

Notice, however, that when the disciples came out of the water dragging the net, there was already a fish on the fire. That fish was the true miracle fish, for it was the one Jesus Himself provided. The fish on the fire may represent Israel, God's miracle nation, which will truly be experiencing the fire of trials and testing in the final days before the Lord's return.

Zechariah wrote of Israel's experience during the Tribulation:

> And it shall come to pass, that in all the land, saith the Lord, two parts therein shall be cut off and die; but

Nations in the Net

the third shall be left therein. And I will bring the third part through the fire, and will refine them as silver is refined, and will try them as gold is tried: they shall call on my name, and I will hear them: I will say, It is my people: and they shall say, The Lord is my God (Zech 13:8,9).

When we subtract Israel from the total membership of the United Nations, there are 153 nations remaining. The parallel is striking: 153 fish in the net, 153 Gentile nations in the United Nations. Of course, it is quite possible that more nations may yet be admitted to the United Nations, but it is also possible that some of the smaller nations in the UN may consolidate. There are current negotiations between the governments of Iraq and Syria to unite their countries as one.

The fact that we introduced this interpretation years ago, when the number of nations was yet considerably below the 153 Gentile UN membership, would indicate it has merit. We suggest that this prophetic overview of God catching the nations of this world into His net adds to the burden of proof that we are indeed living in the last days of the age of man.

In view of this most impressive at-the-door sign, Christians have valid reason to be looking for the soon return of Jesus to call them out of this world to meet Him in the air.

SIX

Russia: Enemy to the North

What has Russia to do with the Bible? The Bible is the only book in all the libraries of the world that gives a complete and accurate survey of Russia's origin, subsequent history, and final judgment. Since Russia at present represents the greatest threat to the free world and the most menacing potential for exterminating the nation of Israel, Bible students must examine Scripture for its complete profile. We will first consider Russia in history and prophecy and then examine the Russian confederacy, or Russia and its allies in the end times.

When we talk about Russia as the first publicly avowed atheistic nation in human history, we should also mention the fact that Russia will be the last nation to exercise an atheistic posture, according to prophecy. Because it is both the first and last nation to take up an avowed rejection of the existence of God, it singles itself out for unique treatment at the hand of God's judgment. We shall examine carefully how God distinguishes Russia from all other nations on earth.

Before doing this we need to discover who the Russian people and nation are. Naturally, we turn to the Bible.

National Origins

The Russian nation and people are first discovered in the table of nations and languages found in Genesis 10 and 11. Ham and his descendants are represented by thirty nations. Shem and his descendants are twenty-six nations in number. When we come to Japheth, whose descendants largely settled in Europe, we have only fourteen nations listed. One of them is called Magog (Gen. 10:2), the progenitor of the people we know today as Russians. The people of Magog dwelt north of the Black Sea.

In addition to Magog, we have in the same remarkable chapter of the Book of Genesis the names of two more groups that are coupled with modern Russia as we know it today. They are Tubal and Meshech (Gen. 10:2 and Ezek. 38:2). The fascinating thing about these two names is that Bible scholars have long linked Tubal with the Asiatic capital of Russia called Tobolsk, and Meshech with the European capital of Russia called Moscow. Moreover, these two Russian capitals are almost always spoken of together in Scripture (the exceptions are Isa. 66:19 and Ps. 120:5).

Tubal and Meshech are in the northeast of Cilicia and in the east of Cappadocia. Even from this very cursory examination of Russia's roots, we can easily and finally link these primary references in the

Bible to the true origins of the modern state of Russia.

Before turning to the Bible's prophetic picture for Russia's future role, let us briefly survey Russia's history.

Early History

Russia's history is surprisingly recent. Slavic tribes only began migrating into Russia from the West in the fifth century. The first Russian state was founded by Scandinavian chieftains in the ninth century. In the thirteenth century, the Mongols overran the country. It recovered under the grand dukes and princes of Muscovy, or Moscow, and by 1480 freed itself from the Mongols. Ivan the Terrible was the first to be formally proclaimed Tsar in 1547. Peter the Great (1682–1725) extended his domain and in 1721 founded the Russian Empire.

Modern History

Present-day Russia is an intriguing study for all prophecy students of the Bible. The one nation that has naturally watched the abnormal growth and expansion of predatory Russia is the nation of Israel, officially established in 1948. Israel has been so absorbed by the role of Russia as blueprinted by the Hebrew prophet Ezekiel that in 1972 they published an arresting set of colored maps entitled "Russian Imperial Power in the Middle East" (The *Jerusalem Post Press*, Jerusalem).

The authors of this remarkably significant publication outline modern Russia's dramatic rise to

Russia: Enemy to the North

world power. With expansion indicated in maps and square miles, it is impossible to miss the intention of the new end-time empire-builders. The mighty Soviet navy, now the largest (numerically) in the world, moves into the strategic Mediterranean Sea through the narrow Turkish Dardanelles from naval bases in the Black Sea. Russia dominates the world's most explosive region in the world—the Middle East, with Israel at the hub—both by a military presence and by political strings. Russian domination has become highly visible since 1972.

The spectacular expansion of Russian hegemony is so critical that as recently as June 7, 1978, President Carter, in a major policy speech at Annapolis, Maryland, told the Soviet Union it "can choose either confrontation or cooperation." Carter spoke against a backdrop of heightened superpower tensions. According to the *Oklahoma City Times* of June 7, 1978,

> Carter told a commencement audience at the U.S. Naval Academy, the Soviets were exploiting instability in Africa as they try to expand their influence. "To the Soviet Union," he said, "detente seems to mean a continuing aggressive struggle for political advantage and increased influence in a variety of ways."

Atheistic Philosophy

Soviet Russia is the very first nation in world history to have a governmental platform based on total atheism. Many ancient nations in history displeased God by adhering to a polytheistic religious outlook, that is, believing in many gods rather than in the one supreme God. God's mercy was extended to polytheistic nations such as Egypt, Assyria, and Babylon. But in Ezekiel 38:3 God emphatically declared: "I am against thee, O Gog."

Joseph Stalin (1879–1953) once arrogantly boasted: "We have deposed the czars of the earth; we shall now dethrone the Lord of Heaven." Even more recently leaders in Moscow have bragged:

> Our rocket has bypassed the moon. It is nearing the sun, and we have not discovered God. We have turned out lights in heaven that no man will be able to put on again. We are breaking the yoke of the Gospel, the opium of the masses. Let us go forth and Christ shall be relegated to mythology.*

Of course, the basic premise of communism is its false atheistic doctrine that there is no God. It is a sobering thing to read in the Bible what God thinks of atheists. We read in Psalms 14:1 and 53:1, "The fool hath said in his heart, There is no God." There are five different Hebrew words in the Bible for "fool," but this one—*nabal*—means not only intellectually wrong, but morally and willfully wrong. It denotes a shamelessly wicked person, an evil character rather than simple folly. The remainder of Ps. 14:1 states: "They are corrupt, they have done abominable works." Obviously, more than folly is implied.

*Rev. Charles Pack, *Prophecy, 1978* (*Thy Kingdom Come* Telecast).

This wickedness is visible in the special decree issued by the Anti-God Council of Moscow when Russia invaded Poland:

> All churches, synagogues, and other religious meeting places are to be closed; the anti-God movement will start founding branches at once in territories occupied by the Red Army; all clergy are suspended; people condemned by the State on account of blasphemy are to be released at once; all laws against anti-God propaganda are to be rescinded; an atheistic paper is to be issued by the Anti-God Council in the Polish language; 2,800,000 rubles are to be set apart for organizing the anti-God movement in Poland, and the Russian Ambassador is to initiate it at once.*

This same kind of diabolical wickedness will be expressed when Russia invades Israel, but the intensity will be worse, because the Jew represents one word to atheistic Russians: God.

Prophecy

Ezekiel, more than any other biblical writer, chronicles the end-time role and final ruin of Russia. The two key chapters are 38 and 39. Gog and Magog are easily identified as referring to Russia. The word "Gog" (Ezek. 38:2,3) is a word for ruler and means "roof" or "man on the top." The term "Russ" has been associated with the Hebrew word *Rosh*, meaning "chief," which occurs in Ezekiel 38:2.

---

*Lehman Strauss, *The End of this Present World* (Grand Rapids, Mich.: Zondervan, 1968), p. 59.

Further, Ezekiel 38:6 refers to "north quarters," which means north of Israel. Moscow is directly north of Jerusalem.

Ezekiel 38:4 states that God is going to put "hooks into thy jaws, and I will bring thee forth." We can easily recognize several hooks: (1) Russia desperately needs a warm-water passage. The waters around Israel offer this. (2) The fabulous mineral and chemical deposits of the Dead Sea are equivalent to four times the wealth of the United States, according to modern computations. (3) The oil deposits of the Middle East are indispensable for the survival and success of modern industrialized nations.

When Will Russia Invade Israel?

This question is on the lips of millions of Bible students. During the Yom Kippur War (October 6–24, 1973), it is reported that all Israel was talking about Gog and Magog. Soldiers on both fronts of that war were asking whether the Hebrew prophets had said anything about the invasion of Israel by Russia.

There are two sets of references to Gog and Magog in prophecy. The first is, of course, Ezekiel 38 and 39. The second is Revelation 20:8. These are not the same war.

The Ezekiel 38–39 references do not indicate that the Messiah is present in the midst of the Jews, although it mentions them being regathered and re-created as a nation. These two chapters refer to the war as taking place after the re-creation of the state of Israel, but before all Jews have been regathered (see Ezek. 38:8; cf. 39:28).

Ezekiel 38:11 refers to "unwalled villages" and gives an indication of time. Older Israelis who have known the pogroms, the Nazi era, and the ghettos consider the present era comparatively secure and free for them. Only in the last century have there been unwalled cities, towns, and villages in Israel.

Ezekiel 38:8,16 gives a clue as to the time framework: "in the latter years" and "in the latter days." This would appear to place this invasion during the Great Tribulation, or possibly just before. In the midst of the seven-year peace treaty period, Russia will trigger the Great Tribulation by breaking the false peace made with the Antichrist and then invading Israel.

One thing is clear in Scripture: At the point when Israel appears to be upon the verge of destruction, God will intervene and the invasion will go up in smoke. Israel will spend seven months burying the dead. Russia will be largely wiped out. The miraculous intervention of God could be by an earthquake or by a nuclear mistake by the Russians. If a ballistic missile were to fall short of its intended target it could destroy millions of Russians.

How Can Russia Mount Such an Invasion?

First of all, Russia's military budget grows steadily, receiving twenty to twenty-five percent of the country's Gross National Product (GNP) every year. The United States spends only five percent of its GNP for military purposes. Russia has more missiles and bombers than the United States. They have twice as many men in arms, four times as many artillery pieces, and significant numerical advantages in helicopters, tactical planes, and submarines. They are no longer afraid of retaliation.

The Results

The overwhelming and devastating defeat of Russia is graphically described in great detail in Ezekiel 38 and 39. Ezekiel 39:2 takes an audit: "I will . . . leave but the sixth part of thee." This is rendered literally, "I will six thee" or even better, "I will afflict thee with six plagues." The plagues are listed in Ezekiel 38:22 as pestilence, blood, overflowing rain, great hailstones, fire, and brimstone. Remember that God also destroyed the abominable cities of Sodom and Gomorrah by fire and brimstone.

The Reason For Judgment

Russia has denied and blasphemed God. God will destroy it "that the heathen may know me" (Ezek. 38:16), that God may "be known in the eyes of many nations, and they shall know that I am the Lord" (Ezek. 38:23), and last but not least, "So the house of Israel shall know that I am the Lord their God from that day and forward" (Ezek. 39:22). From Russia's destruction shall come Israel's national conversion. Once again God will use the wrath of men to praise Him.

Russia's ill-fated final attempt to conquer the world will demonstrate that Russia acted like the fool of Psalm 14:1–like an insane nation. The proof of incurable insanity will be further demonstrated. Revelation 20:7,8 indicates that Russia will be the

Russia: Enemy to the North

final atheistic nation after the Millennium: "And when the thousand years are expired, Satan shall be loosed out of his prison, And shall go out to deceive the nations which are in the four quarters of the earth, Gog and Magog, to gather them together to battle." The first, foremost, and final atheistic nation thus meets its doom.

Thus far we have examined the biblical history of Russia and the prophecy as to its future. Remember that the Hebrew prophet Ezekiel, who outlines the final Russian invasion of Israel in his prophecy, did not even know a nation named Russia in his day. Slavic tribes migrated into Russia only in the fifth century. There was no such thing as a Russian Empire until 1721. Yet with uncanny accuracy he forecasts the end-time rise of this nation that will launch an all-out attack to annihilate Israel.

If President Leonid Brezhnev, current Soviet leader, is not "Gog" then it must almost certainly be his immediate successor who will spearhead the invasion of Israel from the north quarters.

The startling thing is that Russia will not be alone in this attack. Ezekiel faithfully records the names of the principal nations that will be linked together with the Russian bear, so that people living in the end time will not be taken totally by surprise when they see Russia and the huge confederacy roll down toward Israel.

Other Nations

In addition to the nations Ezekiel specifically singled out for active participation in the all-out war for the final destruction of Israel, there will doubtless be other nations backing the Russian northern confederacy. This will likely include some if not all of the present Islamic nations that are united in their animosity against Israel. They appear to have no compunctions about subjugating their Islamic principles to atheistic Russia when it comes to insuring what they believe will be the Israeli annihilation. While it is true that the Islamic nations do not have the military means on their own to defeat Israel (eloquently demonstrated in four wars launched by Islamic enemies of Israel since 1948), they do have petro-dollars and vast reservoirs of oil, without which no modern nation can wage war.

These Islamic enemy countries that surround Israel sprawl across two continents—Africa and Asia. They are from eighty-five to one hundred percent Moslem. Ethiopia and Libya, both specifically named as belonging to the ranks of the Russian invaders, presently have Marxist governments.

The most recent demonstration of how a predominantly Moslem country can willingly subjugate itself to atheistic rulership is Afghanistan. Afghanistan is ninety-nine percent Moslem, but it now has a Communist government. We mention Afghanistan since it clearly demonstrates how an Islamic country can cooperate with atheistic Russia's objectives.

According to the *National Bildzeitung* (West Germany, May 19, 1978), the KGB actually toppled the former Moslem government of Afghanistan. For as long as five years, Afghan officers were trained to become Communist anarchists, according to the report. A trained KGB killer allegedly shot and killed an Afghan Communist leader on April 17, 1978, and blamed President Daoud for this murder. This then gave an excuse for the bombardment of President Daoud's palace. President Daoud was murdered and a trained Communist took over. Afghanistan, a ninety-nine percent Moslem country with a population of twenty million, became overnight the latest Marxist country under Russian dictatorship, despite the fact that Russia is atheist.

East Germany

One of the most sophisticated Russian allies is East Germany. Other than Russia, five specific allies are earmarked for the invasion team. Russia is team captain. Second in command will be East Germany. We read in Ezekiel 38:6 that "Gomer, and all his bands . . ." will move south to the borders of Israel. In the Talmud, Gomer is spoken of as Germani, or the Germans. The major portion of Germany was never connected with the old Roman Empire, and thus it is certain that East Germany will not be part of the revived Roman Empire. The linking of Gomer with Rosh, Meshech, and Tubal clearly indicates that East Germany at least will be allied with Russia in the confederacy that is being formed. In this connection it is significant that East Germany is already linked with Russia.

In the June 19, 1978, *Newsweek* we read about the East German "Afrika Korps."

> At a recent performance by the Cuban National Ballet in Washington, a Cuban diplomat spotted an American acquaintance. "I don't know why you keep harping about Africa to us," he complained.

"Why don't you look at the Germans?" He had a point. East Germany has stationed about 4,500 soldiers in Africa, and an equal number of security officers and civilian advisers. East Germany's "Afrika Korps" performs so efficiently that it has won disproportionate influence in a dozen radical African states and liberation movements. "The East Germans are actually the stabilizing force for the Marxist-Leninist regimes in Africa," says a high-ranking West German intelligence officer. "The Cubans are the cannon fodder."

These elite Russian allies of the end time are code-named "Brotherhood in Arms." According to the *Newsweek* article, the East German Defense Minister Heinz Hoffmann visited Angola just before the Katangans launched their invasion of Zaire. The East German officers planned the attack and sent tanks to the Angolan border to protect the retreating Katangans. These German Afrika Korps run three training camps near the Zairian border, and another 1,000 soldiers are attached to the Angolan army. East German pilots fly missions against anti-government guerillas. The East Germans have secret police in most of Africa's Marxist nations. Most ominous of all is the fact that East Germans are training members of the Palestine Liberation Organization to fly modern warplanes.

Iran

Another Russian confederate in the war against Israel will be Iran, called Persia in Ezekiel 38:5. Iran will be one of the most strategic of Russia's allies in that war. The Russians are looking to the Middle East

Russia: Enemy to the North

for oil supplies. This prospect deeply worries Pentagon planners, who fear that Soviet involvement in the Horn of Africa stems from Moscow's desire to control choke points along the tanker routes that carry oil to Western markets.

Marxist revolutionaries played a major role in the toppling of Iran's monarchy and are demanding a larger role in the government of the Ayatollah Khomeini. The Ayatollah is not a Marxist and is not pro-Russian. He is, however, anti-Israel. It is not difficult to imagine his aligning himself with Russia against Israel. Also worth consideration is the revolutionary government's apparent difficulty in bringing stability to Iran. If that instability continues, the Persian plum may be ripe for harvest by Russian expansionism.

It is widely speculated that information about U.S. secret military weapons deployed in Iran may have fallen into Russian hands. An editorial in the March 9, 1979, *Daily Oklahoman* observes in part:

> The American-equipped Iranian armed forces are the most modern east of Suez. As long as the shah's government controlled them, they were no threat to Israel. But if they arrayed with the Soviet-armed forces of Syria and Iraq in an attack on Israel, even if Jordan and Saudi Arabia should remain out of the conflict, they could partially nullify the advantages to be won by a treaty with Egypt.

Ethiopia

Another victim in the Russian push for power is Ethiopia, specifically named in Ezekiel 38:5. A couple of simmering wars in Ethiopia exploded early in 1978. A Soviet airlift of arms, vast numbers of Russian advisers, and the land of Ethiopia became a major battlefield. The strategic Horn of Africa represents high stakes. The world's most precious commodity—black gold—enters the dramatic picture because the shipping routes through the Red Sea and Indian Ocean now command Russia's interest.

Huge Russian Ilyushin transport planes and the big Antonov Russian planes wheeled into Addis Ababa airport, in the Ethiopian capital. They dumped over $850 million worth of arms, including T-34 tanks, field guns, heavy mortars, and light missiles. Fighter planes, including the advanced MiG-23, were exported from Russian bases to Ethiopia late in 1977 and early in 1978. The Russians are planning to establish a navy base at Massawa, even though they already have naval and air facilities in both South Yemen and Aden just across the Red Sea.

Russia has thus conquered Ethiopia, and it is ready to use Ethiopia in the four-pronged attack on Israel described in Ezekiel 38 and 39.

Libya

Besides East Germany, Iran, and Ethiopia, Libya and Turkey are included in the Russian confederacy. Libya is an oil-producing country, and therefore has a powerful lever in its hands. It is not a small country. It is 700,000 square miles larger than our state of Alaska. It is an intensely Moslem country. The dictator of Libya is General El-Qaddafi, an arrogant, bitterly anti-Israeli ruler. Bible prophecy has placed Libya with its oil in the Russian camp. It has intimate political ties with Russia, and Russia has sold it many billion dollars' worth of advanced arms annually since 1975. The Libyans threw out the American Wheelus Air Force Base and substituted Russian aid. Clearly the Bible is right in placing the Libyans on the Russian confederate team.

Turkey

This leaves Turkey as the fifth nation of the Russian confederacy. Ezekiel 38:6 states that "the house of Togarmah . . . and all his bands" will join Russia. This is Turkey. The Turks are described as coming from "the uttermost north," and they spring from the Turkoman tribes of central Asia. They reside in modern Turkey and Armenia. Thus southern Russia, with its Cossacks, and Turkey are banded tightly together.

When Turkey invaded the island of Cyprus in the Mediterranean, the U.S. Congress cut off the sale of arms to Turkey. A deep rift was formed between Turkey and the United States. Although that rift is being mended, the Turks are becoming more friendly with the Russians. The Turkish foreign minister has signed a political document for friendly relations and cooperation between Russia and Turkey that foreshadows the Russian confederacy of the last days.

In 1973, the Turks completed a strategic bridge across the Bosporus, which unites the continents of Asia and Europe. It is the largest single-span bridge in Europe, looming ten stories high. Russian armor and troops could pour over this bridge to join with Turkey against Israel. For thirty centuries men sought to span this ancient strait, but it was completed only seven years ago in 1973.

Russian aggression is rapidly gathering a confederacy of nations to march against Israel, just as Ezekiel prophesied. Modern-day events are focusing the full impact of these prophecies on our generation. The nations are aligning themselves. When Russia, the largest country in the world, links up with East Germany, Iran, Ethiopia, Libya, and Turkey, more than 400 million humans will pursue this defiance of God and march against the nation that owes its founding and present existence to its special relationship with Jehovah.

SEVEN
The Mystery of Babylon

On March 13, 1978, after a breakfast of Iraqi bread and fig preserves served with a small cup of black, bitter, thick coffee, the ninety-seven members of the Southwest Radio Church tour group boarded buses and headed for Babylon.

From Baghdad on the Tigris River we traveled sixty-five miles southwest over a modern four-lane highway to the site of ancient Babylon on the Euphrates. The land is very flat and fertile.

The first trace of the ancient city was the ruins of the palace of the queen of Babylon. Being a Persian, she longed for the mountains of her native land, so Nebuchadnezzar built a high hill and erected a palace on the summit for his wife. Next we passed the theatre (much of which has already been restored) where the king and his court were entertained. We passed a hotel—rather small by American standards—and came to the part of the ruins that is presently being restored.

As we stood between the Ishtar Gate and the lion pit and surveyed the scene—part restoration and part desolation—we wondered if this would be the Babylon mentioned in Revelation 18, or if we should look for another possible candidate.

Babylon—Then and Now

Students of Bible prophecy have listed more than one hundred end-time prophecies that are visibly being fulfilled today. These prophecies concern the refounding of Israel as a nation, the rise of Russia to the north, the knowledge explosion, earthquakes, astrology, witchcraft, the revived Roman Empire, the world armament race, and many others. That Babylon will be destroyed ultimately and completely just before Christ returns is also clearly prophesied. Some have debated whether the Babylon of Revelation 18 will be a religious system or a nation that would be comparable to ancient Babylon. But as other apocalyptic prophecies come into view, waiting for the revival of Babylon has been as frustrating as looking in vain for the key piece in a jigsaw puzzle.

On March 29, 1971, a news release from Beirut, Lebanon, announced a plan by the government of Iraq to rebuild Babylon with its great walls and hanging gardens according to its "original architectural designs." The news item stated: "Iraq says it plans to rebuild the ancient city of Babylon, whose hanging gardens were among the seven wonders of the world. The project will cost about $30 million."

To understand the magnitude of such a giant undertaking, let us consider this brief description of Babylon, from the days of Nimrod. It grew in size and importance, century after century, until it

The Mystery of Babylon

reached its greatest glory in the reign of Nebuchadnezzar in 604–562 B.C. As described by Greek historian Herodotus:

> It was an exact square of 15 miles on a side, or 60 miles around and was surrounded by a brick wall 87 feet thick and 350 feet high . . . on the wall were 250 towers, and the top of the wall was wide enough to allow 6 chariots to drive abreast. Twenty-five magnificent avenues, 150 feet wide, ran across the city from north to south, and the same number crossed them at right angles from east to west, making 676 great squares, each nearly three-fifths of a mile on a side. The city was divided into two equal parts by the River Euphrates, that flowed diagonally though it, and whose banks within the city were walled up, and pierced with brazen gates, with steps leading down to the river. At the ends of the main avenues, on each side of the city, were gates, whose leaves were of brass, and that shone as they were opened or closed in the rising or setting sun, like leaves of flame . . . near one of the palaces stood the tower of Bel, or Babel, consisting of eight towers, each 75 feet high, rising one upon the other, with an outside winding stairway to its summit, which towers, with the chapel on the top, made a height of 660 feet.*

Such an undertaking by the government of Iraq would not have been even remotely possible thirty years ago. Before 1950, all the Arab countries com-

*Francis R. Godolphin, trans., *The Greek Historians: The Complete and Unabridged Works of Herodotus, Thucydides, Xenophon and Arrian* (New York: Random House, 1942).

bined could not have restored Nebuchadnezzar's footstool without foreign aid. The event that has changed the poorest of nations into the richest and made possible the rebuilding of Babylon was the discovery of oil in the Middle East. However, it was readily apparent from the beginning of the restoration that the initial $30 million would only be a drop in the Euphrates River. The United Nations Educational, Scientific, and Cultural Organization (UNESCO) later appropriated $35 million for the project, and other contributions have come from individual oil-rich Arabs.

In considering the 225 square miles of ruins that once was the city of Babylon, it was our own personal observation that after six years, not more than five or ten percent of the city has been restored. A representative of the government of Iraq assured us that by 1982 all of ancient Babylon would be again as it was in the days of Nebuchadnezzar. If the government of Iraq gets behind the project with more men and material, the goal probably could be reached.

A large portion of the ancient city of Babylon lies thirty to fifty feet below the surface of the ground. This condition was caused by the shifting of the Euphrates' riverbed and blowing sand during the dry seasons over the past 2,000 years. However, some foundations are still almost at ground level. The bricks in the buildings are in excellent condition, even after 2,500 years. But only the portions of the buildings beneath the ground remain because, like most ancient buildings in that area, the stones and bricks have been removed for dwellings and other purposes.

The walls of Nineveh and many of its buildings were built out of stones that were floated down the Tigris River from 100 to 200 miles away. But such building material was not available to Nebuchadnezzar unless transported overland, an almost impossible task. There are almost no trees or stones at all in the Mesopotamian Valley, an area about 500 miles long and 100 miles wide. Therefore, the only material available to the Tower of Babel builders, and later the builders of Babylon, was brick.

We read of the building of the Tower of Babel in Genesis 11:2,4:

> And it came to pass, as they journeyed from the east, that they found a plain in the land of Shinar; and they dwelt there. And they said one to another, Go to, let us make brick, and burn them throughly. And they had brick for stone, and slime had they for morter. And they said, Go to, let us build us a city and a tower, whose top may reach unto heaven.

Moses, who had never seen the Tower of Babel, noted by inspiration of God that they burned the brick "throughly," and indeed they did. The huge Ziggurat at Ur is made of bricks and is still in excellent condition after 4,000 years.

Archaeologists have also removed portions of buildings. We were informed while in Babylon that a large portion of the Ishtar Gate was removed and reassembled in Germany. But let us think for a moment about the billions and billions of bricks it must have taken to build a city 225 miles square with high, monstrous brick walls all around it. At least half, and possibly two thirds of the ruins will have to be restored with new bricks. Until now it would have been impossible for the government of Iraq to provide this enormous quantity of bricks.

In traveling from Baghdad to Babylon we saw scores of new brick factories going full blast, and others are also being built to the north and south of Baghdad along the highways and railroad tracks. Although much of the brick output of these factories is being used for new construction, large shipments are being channeled to Babylon. All the output could be diverted to the restoration project when needed. The slime pits of both Babel and Babylon that yield tar or bitumen are still in evidence. Vast amounts lie just beneath the surface throughout the area.

For the first time since the decline and fall of Babylon, material is available for its complete restoration. Funds have become available through the sale of oil, and as the wealth of the world gradually shifts back to the Middle East there is both reason and incentive for the rebuilding of this once-proud metropolis.

When the government of Iraq announced that it planned to rebuild Babylon, the world stage was further prepared for the entrance of the two main characters—Christ and the Antichrist. Every prominent forerunner of the Antichrist has built a great city. Cain went out from the presence of God and built a city. Nimrod built Babel. Nebuchadnezzar made Babylon the jewel of the world. Nero desired to rebuild Rome as an eternal city. (We must wonder if Babel, and later Babylon, was not the site of Cain's

The Mystery of Babylon

city, since many would-be world rulers besides Nimrod and Nebuchadnezzar desired the site.) Alexander planned to restore Babylon to make it the capital city of his vast empire. God stopped Alexander through an early death, and when we were in Babylon we saw the memorial column that was erected on the site where he died. Napoleon drew up plans to rebuild Babylon, but God stopped him at Waterloo.

According to Bible typology, the Antichrist will in all probability have a city. The city of the last world ruler before Jesus Christ returns is described in Isaiah 13 and 14. The setting for this prophecy is given in Isaiah 13:6,9–11:

> Howl ye; for the day of the Lord is at hand; it shall come as a destruction from the Almighty. . . . Behold, the day of the Lord cometh, cruel both with wrath and fierce anger, to lay the land desolate; and he shall destroy the sinners thereof out of it. For the stars of heaven and the constellations thereof shall not give their light: the sun shall be darkened in his going forth, and the moon shall not cause her light to shine. And I will punish the world for their evil.

The obvious conclusion is that the time set forth by Isaiah is at the return of Jesus Christ. In verses 3–5, the prophet even described the coming of the Lord with the armies of heaven. The city upon which God will vent His fiercest anger in that day is Babylon (Isa. 13). In verse 19 we read: "Babylon, the glory of kingdoms, the beauty of the Chaldees' excellency, shall be as when God overthrew Sodom and Gomorrah."

Isaiah was referring to that monstrous mound of ruins on the bank of the Euphrates River that has been partially restored today.

Many Old Testament prophecies have a dual application. In Isaiah 13, the conquest of Babylon by the Medes is mentioned. But Isaiah's prophecy goes beyond the Median conquest to the final and ultimate destruction of Babylon when the Lord will come in judgment at the end of the age. We read in Isaiah 13:20: "[Babylon] shall never be inhabited, neither shall it be dwelt in from generation to generation: neither shall the Arabian pitch tent there; neither shall the shepherds make their fold there."

Isaiah predicted a time when Babylon would never be inhabited by anyone again. But to this date, the city has never ceased to exist in some form since its founding. When the combined armies of the Medes and Persians conquered Babylon in 538 B.C. as described in Daniel 5, they diverted the Euphrates River into a network of canals and marched into the city at night through the riverbed. The major portion of the Babylonian army was on the wall. Caught by surprise, the armed forces of Belshazzar, the Babylonian king, were quickly overcome. Little damage was done to the city proper, and it remained an important city in the Babylonian province of the Medo-Persian Empire.

In Alexander's day Babylon was still a powerful city, and it remained so until Seleucus, one of Alexander's generals, founded a nearby city that drew off much of the population.

As late as A.D. 60, the apostle Peter was ministering to the descendants of the Jews in Babylon who did not return to Israel after the Babylonian captivity (1 Pet. 5:13).

In the middle of the fifth century, Theodoret wrote that Babylon was inhabited only by Jews and that three Jewish universities were still maintained there to serve the large Jewish population of the city and surrounding areas.

In A.D. 917, Ibu Hanket mentioned Babylon as an insignificant village, but still in existence.

In the twelfth century, Babylon was somewhat revived under the Moslem name "Two Mosques."

In 1900, Babylon—or Hillah as it was then called—had a population of about 10,000.

When we were in Babylon recently, we visited a modest hotel, a museum, and passed rows of houses and tents within the old city limits. A number of children were in evidence, and we can say that at least a part of old Babylon is still inhabited today. Thus the prophecy of Isaiah that Babylon will be destroyed like Sodom and Gomorrah, never to be inhabited again, has not yet come to pass. The fact that the final judgment of Babylon is yet to come is evident from Revelation 18:17-24, where John prophesied that Babylon would be destroyed finally and completely in one hour by a fiery judgment.

Babylon, however, was not just a nation, a political order, an empire, or a religion—it was a system. Babylonian society as a whole worked together to produce a system, comprised of the following parts:

The Nation. The nation of Babylon was approximately 600 miles long and 200 miles wide. The land, even as it is today, was the richest and most productive in the world. Good land is a necessity for the expansion of any nation into empire status. The strength of Egypt, for example, lies in the fertile Nile Valley. Although the land of Babylon produced no lumber, nor was stone readily available, it was good for making bricks. As in Egypt, water was available from two great rivers—the Euphrates on the west and the Tigris on the east.

The City. The hub of the nation was the city of Babylon, which surpassed even mighty Nineveh in beauty, size, and glory. Without doubt, up to that time it was the crowning achievement of mankind (Dan. 4:30). The mighty city of Babylon filled every subject of the nation with awe and fanatical patriotism.

The Religion. The nation was unified by the religion of the Chaldeans. The priests of this mystical religious order practiced divination and astrology. The goal of Babylon's religion was to direct all devotion and service to the king, and the ecclesiastical order maintained its favored position only as long as Nebuchadnezzar could use it for his own purposes.

The Political Structure. In Babylon all governmental authority was vested in an absolute dictator. The only rights any citizen of Babylon had were the rights given by decree of the king. Nebuchadnezzar had complete power and authority over every person, all land, all property, and even the beasts of the field and the fowls of the air.

The Military. The army of Babylon was the best-trained and best-equipped of any in the world at that time. Judah was fearful of testing its own armed forces and the walls of Jerusalem against Nebuchadnezzar's forces. Nebuchadnezzar's generals were faithful in duty and service to the king.

The Empire. The system propelled the domination of Babylon from Egypt to India—over practically all of the known, civilized world. Wherever the power of Babylon prevailed, the nations were robbed of gold, silver, precious stones, and merchandise of every kind. Rulers of other nations were executed. Princes were made eunuchs. Scientists and other well-educated men and women were taken back to Babylon to work for the king. Everyone was forced to learn the language of the Chaldeans.

As far as the known world of the day was concerned, there was a world church, a world empire, a world ruler, and all nations within the boundaries of Babylon were commanded to worship one man as the supreme god.

The Last Babylon

The last world empire, over which the Antichrist will reign, is compared to ancient Babylon and the Babylonian system in Revelation 17, 18, and 19:1-6. The parallels are as follows:

The Nation. Some believe the Antichrist will be an Assyrian, based on Micah 5:1-6, where the birth of the Messiah is prophesied. In verses 4-6 of this same chapter it is also prophesied that the Messiah would, in the end of the age, deliver Israel from the Assyrian, and that the land of Assyria and the land of

Nimrod (Babylon) would be made waste. The most generally accepted opinion, however, is that the Antichrist will rise up out of the revived Roman Empire of Europe.

The Religion. Just like the state religion of old, when everyone was commanded to worship Nebuchadnezzar as God, so will the world church of the Tribulation period command everyone to worship the Antichrist or be killed (Rev. 11–18). In fact, the world church is called "Mystery Babylon" in Revelation 17:5.

The City. That the Antichrist will have a great city as headquarters for his world government is beyond question. The Bible identifies that city as Babylon in Revelation 18:21: "Thus with violence shall that great city Babylon be thrown down, and shall be found no more at all."

The Political Structure. Although the Antichrist will rise up out of a small nation, a prophecy in Revelation 17:12,13 indicates that an alliance of ten nations will back him, and he will be given great power and authority. According to Daniel 11:41–43 and Revelation 13:7, the Antichrist will be dictator over all races, languages, and nations. Like Nebuchadnezzar, his power will be absolute, and every person on earth will be commanded by the world church to worship him or be killed (Rev. 13:8,15). And just as Nebuchadnezzar had power over all property, the Antichrist will claim ownership over all the riches of the world, including all items of trade and commerce (Dan. 11:43; Rev. 13:16,17).

The Military: During the last half of the Tribulation, the Antichrist will control all the armed forces of the world. The armies of all nations will be gathered together in one army to fight against Jesus Christ and the armies of God when the Lord comes back to earth (Zech. 14:1,2; Rev. 16:12–16; 19:19).

The Last World Empire: The same system Nebuchadnezzar used to extend Babylon over most of the known world will be employed by the Antichrist to extend his power and control over all the earth. As we have already pointed out, the system will include a mighty city, a powerful alliance of nations, a world church, a world dictator, a world army, and the pooling of all the scientific minds of the world to produce a method of controlling all people, trade, and commerce.

It was the dream of Nebuchadnezzar to extend his empire over all the earth and to perpetuate his kingdom forever, and the Antichrist will succeed in some points where the former king failed. But we read of the empire of the Antichrist and his alliance of kings in Daniel 2:44: "And in the days of these kings shall the God of heaven set up a kingdom, which shall never be destroyed: and the kingdom shall not be left to other people . . . it shall stand for ever."

Therefore, we begin to understand the mystery of Babylon as it relates to the coming kingdom of the Antichrist—and its complete destruction by Jesus Christ when He returns.

The United States As the Last Babylon

There are fundamental and conservative Bible scholars who suggest that the United States is the last

Babylon, and their prophetic propositions deserve serious consideration. S. Franklin Logsdon, former pastor of Moody Church in Chicago, has proposed this possibility. Some of the reasons Logsdon and others believe that the United States could be the last Babylon are as follows:

(1) At Babel, God divided mankind into races, languages, and nations to prevent the combining of skills and resources so as to thwart their rebellion against divine authority. Nebuchadnezzar brought the scientific minds of the world together again and taught them a common language (Dan. 1:4). Babylon tried to reverse what God did at Babel, and here in the United States we have done the same thing. People from every race and nation have come into this nation, learned a common language, and pooled their education and skills to produce a technical, scientific society unparalleled in world history.

(2) According to Joel 3 and many other prophetic Scriptures, the nations will be armed for the Battle of Armageddon in the last days. In Jeremiah 50:23–25, the prophet is evidently referring to the last Babylon. God says that this nation will be his armory for the whole world. The world's arms traffic this past year amounted to $400 billion, and the United States accounted for more than half of this amount.

(3) The identifying international emblem of the United States is the Statue of Liberty. But also nearby to the approaches to New York City on Long Island is another possible identifying symbol—Babylon. Babylon, New York is a fairly large city made up of Babylon, North Babylon, and West Babylon—big enough to have three zip codes. In

fact, the entire New York City complex, long hailed as the greatest city in the world, is known as the "Babylon on the Hudson."

(4) Concerning "Mystery Babylon," the United States is the headquarters for the apostate world church movement. Also, the movement for world government through organizations like the Council on Foreign Relations is headquartered in the United States. The United Nations is also in New York City.

(5) We read of the last days in Jeremiah 51:7: "Babylon hath been a golden cup in the Lord's hand, that made all the earth drunken: the nations have drunken of her wine; therefore the nations are mad." The corresponding prophecy is given in Revelation 18:3: ". . . all nations have drunk of the wine of the wrath of her fornication." Almost everywhere you go in the world today, American movies and television programs are shown—displaying and encouraging loose morals and defiance of God's laws.

(6) God gives a warning before the destruction of the last Babylon: "Come out of her, my people, that ye be not partakers of her sins, and that ye receive not of her plagues. For her sins have reached unto heaven, and God hath remembered her iniquities" (Rev. 18:4,5). The warning given here is not for Christians, because the church will already have been caught up to heaven. Israel is called God's earthly people again after the church is raptured, so the reference here must be to Israelites. New York City alone has a larger Jewish population than all of the modern nation of Israel, so it could be God's call for the Jews to leave America.

There are many more reasons given by Logsdon and others why the last Babylon could be the United States. It is obvious that our country has a prominent role in preparing the world for the last Babylonian system. But while we must keep open minds as these end-time prophecies come into focus, we still believe that as we see the wealth of the world shifting back to the Middle East, the Arab nations arming themselves with more powerful weapons than ever, and plans by the government of Iraq to restore the ancient city of Babylon by 1982, restored Babylon is still the most likely candidate to be the city destroyed by fire in one hour as prophesied in Revelation 18.

Babylon—the Counterfeit City

Satan is identified throughout Scripture as the great counterfeiter, and it is obvious that Satan's man, the Antichrist, will attempt to offer the world a counterfeit of the New Jerusalem. Consider the fact that Babylon was a four-square city, 15 miles on each side. The new Jerusalem will also be four-square, but 1,500 miles on each side. The Euphrates River divided the city of Babylon and brought the water essential for physical life to its inhabitants. The River of Life will run through the midst of the New Jerusalem, bringing everlasting life to its celestial inhabitants.

The gates of flaming brass that shone as the sun will be restored in rebuilt Babylon, but brass speaks of judgment. Surely the judgment of the last Babylon was predetermined in the councils of almighty God. The gates of the New Jerusalem will be made of giant pearls, and in contrast to brass—signifying judgment—pearls are symbolic of God's mercy and grace (Matt. 7:6). The hanging gardens, one of the seven wonders of the ancient world, are to be restored to give the city an extraterrestrial appearance. But God will hang the New Jerusalem like a gleaming chandelier in the sky, and the nations on earth will walk in its light (Rev. 21,22).

Babylon remains mysterious among the prophetic signs of Christ's return. It appears evident that the great city will be destroyed in the last days, yet in order to be destroyed it must first be rebuilt. As we have noted, construction on that project is progressing, though rather slowly. It is not for us to be dogmatic about the exact place of Babylon in the total picture. Still, we believe that Babylon will be rebuilt for the Antichrist and later destroyed by the returning Christ.

There is no doubt that prophecy students of seventy-five or one hundred years ago (who would not have had the benefit of the current world situation) would find meaningless many of the signs that cause us to rejoice today. As the time of Christ's return has drawn nearer, the importance of various events on God's prophetic timetable have become increasingly clear. It will almost certainly be the same with Babylon. As Christ's return draws nearer, the mystery of Babylon will become clearer.

EIGHT

The Parade of Planets

> And there shall be signs in the sun, and in the moon, and in the stars; and upon the earth distress of nations, with perplexity; the sea and the waves roaring; Men's hearts failing them for fear, and for looking after those things which are coming on the earth: for the powers of heaven shall be shaken. And then shall they see the Son of man coming in a cloud with power and great glory (Luke 21:25-27).

In the days immediately preceding the return of Jesus Christ there will be spectacular changes in the sun, moon, and stars. Since World War II, prophetic Bible scholars, comparing the signs of the times with existing world conditions, have warned that we are approaching the Tribulation prophesied by Jesus Christ. "For then shall be great tribulation, such as was not since the beginning of the world to this time, no, nor ever shall be" (Matt. 24:21).

In the late 1960s John Gribbin, physical sciences editor of the British magazine *Nature*, and Stephen Plagemann, researcher at NASA's Goddard Space Center in Maryland, began to study the possible ef-

The Parade of Planets

fects of the planetary alignment projected for 1982. In that year all nine planets in our solar system will be in approximate alignment. An imaginary line drawn from the center of the sun to the center of the most distant planet would pass through or near other planets. In their book *The Jupiter Effect,* Gribbin and Plagemann published their scientific conclusions. A review of the book in the September 16, 1974, issue of *Newsweek* stated, "As the planets move into alignment in 1982, their gravitational pull may cause huge storms on the sun. These storms could alter wind directions on earth, reducing the speed of the planet's rotation and triggering serious earthquakes." The article continued, listing conditions the two scientists predicted could be present by 1982:

(1) A great increase in magnetic activity on the sun. Huge storms, sunspots, and solar flares will occur.

(2) The ionosphere may be seriously affected, with great changes occurring in the earth's atmosphere.

(3) Radio and television communications will be disrupted.

(4) Unusual visual effects from the northern lights will burst through the sky.

(5) Wind directions will be changed.

(6) Rainfall and temperature patterns will be greatly altered.

(7) The earth's rotation could be affected, and the length of days changed.

(8) Earthquake activity will increase dramatically.

The two scientists warn that by 1982, "There will be many earthquakes, large and small. . . . And one region where the greatest fault system lies today under a great strain, long overdue for a giant leap forward and just waiting the necessary kick, is California."

The nine planets in our solar system appear on one side of the sun every 179 years. However, the astronomical effect upon the earth's environmental conditions and the sun's activity depends upon the degree of alignment. In view of the frightening projections of these two scientists, let us look at the cosmic conditions prophesied by the Bible for the time shortly before Christ's return.

The Sun

Jesus said, "Immediately after the tribulation of those days shall the sun be darkened" (Matt. 24:29).

The apostle John was shown an apocalyptic vision of the world during the last days of the Great Tribulation. He wrote that because of the sun "men were scorched with great heat" (Rev. 16:9).

The prophet Isaiah wrote, ". . . the light of the sun shall be sevenfold, as the light of seven days" (Isa. 30:26).

The prophet Joel predicted that when the great and terrible day of the Lord would come, "The sun shall be turned into darkness" (Joel 2:31).

For many years astronomers concluded that our sun could maintain its present heat/energy output for at least five billion more years, because its hydrogen supply is only about half exhausted. More recently, some astronomers have reappraised this theory. They now believe that once a star has expended half its hydrogen, it is in danger of experiencing a nova—getting brighter and hotter for a period of seven to fourteen days, and then becoming darker. Larger stars supernova—blow up. Smaller stars, like our own sun, nova. There are about twenty-three novas a year in the observable universe.

Some astronomers now believe that the increased sunspot activity of recent years is a preliminary sign that our sun is about to nova. The increase in solar activity predicted for 1982 could be just the trigger that would set off the atomic collapse of the sun. The nova of our sun would almost assuredly cause the sun to (1) become unusually bright, as Isaiah prophesied, (2) become much hotter, as John prophesied, and (3) become dark, as Joel and Jesus prophesied. A nova of our sun would mean the end of life on earth as we know it.

The Moon

Isaiah prophesied that "the light of the moon shall be as the light of the sun" (Isa. 30:26).

Joel said that "the moon [shall be turned] into blood" (Joel 2:31).

Jesus said that "the moon shall not give her light" (Matt. 24:29).

Inasmuch as the moon has no light source of its own and only reflects the sun's light, the prophetic passages are in complete harmony with science. It naturally follows that when the sun becomes seven times brighter, the moon's reflective light will make the night as hot and as bright as an average day. Then, when the sun becomes dark, the moon will reflect no light at all. As for the moon's turning to blood, scientists believe there will be strange lighting effects in 1982. These could explain a temporary reddening of the moon's glow.

The Earth

The environmental changes in the earth during the Tribulation, those last seven years before Christ's return, will be varied and severe. Consider the following possibilities.

Scripture indicates that terrible storms and floods will occur. Ezekiel 38, the chapter that chronicles the great Russian invasion of Israel, also mentions great hailstones and an overflowing rain. Revelation 16:21 says that men will be struck down by "a great hail out of heaven, every stone about the weight of a talent." A talent is the equivalent of one hundred pounds. Upper atmospheric disturbances such as those predicted for 1982 could cause such terrible storms.

Drought is another condition prophesied for the last days. It is also an expected result of the conditions described by Gribbin and Plagemann. We have already noted that a long-range weather study commissioned by the CIA predicts drought and famine in the years to come. Weather conditions over the past decade have become increasingly unpredictable. Record temperature extremes have become the rule rather than the exception.

The Parade of Planets

The alignment of planets will take place over a period of several years. The earth circles the sun every 365.25 days. The trip around the sun determines our yearly cycle of seasons. However, the planets farther from the sun require more time to complete their cycles. Pluto requires 248 earth years to make a solar cycle. This means that the planets are already lining up, and this could be a factor in the world's changing weather patterns.

The March, 1976, edition of the prestigious *Smithsonian* magazine carried the following apocalyptic warning: "The world as we know it will likely be ruined before the year 2000. . . . The momentum toward tragedy is at this moment so great that there is probably no way of halting it. . . . No amount of scientific wizardry or improved weather will change this situation."

As far back as 1973, Reid Bryson, director of the University of Wisconsin's Environmental Institute, warned: "This evidence is now abundantly clear that the climate of earth is changing in a direction that is not good."

All this is predicted in the Bible for the last days. Christians will want to keep their eyes on this parade of planets scheduled for 1982, if indeed the rapture of the Church-Age believers has not already occurred by that time.

Time will also be affected during the last days. Speaking of the Great Tribulation, Jesus said, "And except those days should be shortened, there should no flesh be saved: but for the elect's sake those days shall be shortened" (Matt. 24:22). God has already established the duration of the Tribulation period. It will continue for seven years—no more, no less. In terms of the calendar, the Tribulation cannot be shortened. Therefore, it seems that Jesus was referring to the days themselves. The actual days will be shortened in length.

At first suggestion the concept seems preposterous. But both Scripture and science support the idea. We are told in Revelation 8:12 that "the day shone not for a third part of it, and the night likewise." This verse does not suggest a temporary darkening of the sun, as occurred at Christ's crucifixion, but a shortening by one-third of both the day and the night.

An Associated Press release dated May 6, 1973, stated:

> A giant storm on the sun last year . . . slowed the spinning of the earth for one long day. . . . Dr. Stephen Plagemann of the Goddard Space Flight Center and Dr. John Gribbin, an astronomer, reached their conclusions after studying the biggest solar storm ever recorded. . . . They discovered that on August 8 the daily increase in the length of the day was ten times greater than would have been expected at that time of the year.

The year 1982 could witness the fulfillment of Jesus' remarkable prophecy that the days would be shortened.

The earth's polar alignment could also be affected by the events of the last days. It is possible that before the Flood rain did not fall on the earth. The ground may have been watered by a mist. A layer of

The Parade of Planets

water vapor in the upper atmosphere may have served as an air conditioner, causing nearly even temperatures from pole to pole and screening out dangerous cosmic and ultraviolet rays. When this vapor canopy collapsed at the Flood, the earth tilted twenty-three degrees on its axis and a great amount of this water was frozen at the ice caps. The resulting change in environment decreased the average life span of man from several hundred years to threescore and ten.*

According to Gribbin and Plagemann, the earth will experience tremendous gravitational pull from other planets during the 1982 lineup. Under such stress it would not be unreasonable to see the earth's axis position change. Isaiah 24:20 says, "The earth shall reel to and fro like a drunkard." It is possible that at the alignment of planets in 1982, the earth could be righted on its axis and pre-Flood conditions restored. We are informed by Scripture that during the millennial reign of Christ, all deterrents to a fruitful earth will be removed, and people will again live to be several hundred years old (Isa. 65:19-25).

Earthquakes, which will play an important part in the drama of the last days, could be another of the results of the 1982 parade of planets. Jesus said that earthquakes would increase in the last days as a sign for men to repent and be saved. Three major earthquakes will come during the Tribulation, according to the Book of Revelation. One will be so

---

*Donald Wesley Patten, *The Biblical Flood and the Ice Epoch* (Seattle, Wash.: Pacific Meridian Publishing Co., 1966), ch. "The Greenhouse Effect."

strong that it will shake and destroy every wall built by man, level mountains, and make islands sink into the sea (Ezek. 38:20; Rev. 16:19–21).

Compare these prophecies to the warnings issued by Gribbin and Plagemann:

> We can predict this apocalyptic date within a couple of years. A remarkable chain of evidence, much of it known for decades but never before linked together, points to 1982 as the year . . . the most massive earthquakes known in the populated regions of the Earth [will occur]. . . . At the end point of the chain, directly causing this disaster, is a rare alignment of the planets in the Solar system. . . . There is no question about the implication.

Some have criticized the conclusions of Gribbin and Plagemann on the basis that the gravitational pull on the earth would not be great enough to cause earthquakes as mentioned in *The Jupiter Effect*. It is not the direct gravitational pull on the *earth* that is important, but rather the pull on the *sun* that will result in activity on the solar surface that will bring reactions on earth. A scientific study revealed that when Mercury is in conjunction with one or more of the inner planets—Venus, Earth, Mars, or Jupiter—solar activity increases. Solar storms are one of the causes of earthquakes, and they also affect the weather.

Others have objected that a literal linking of solar activity with the prophesied signs in the heavens is not valid, because such an interpretation limits the power of God to perform special miracles.

We maintain that the Bible, accurately predicting such solar activity thousands of years before it happens, is a special miracle in itself. Such prophecy proves that God is the Master of His creation, with the liberty to use established scientific laws to accomplish His purposes if He so desires.

Admittedly, as with the introduction of any relatively new scientific theory, there is wide disagreement among scientists themselves concerning the Gribbin-Plagemann projections for the next alignment of planets. Some contend there will be no effect on either the sun or the earth. But there is some evidence from past alignments. In *The Long Day of Joshua and Six Other Catastrophies,* the authors quote ancient Roman literature that reported that when the planets lined up on Jove (Jupiter) there were lightning bolts in the heavens and a shaking of the earth.

To defend or discount the theory of Gribbin and Plagemann is not our purpose. Our only interest is to compare the two scientists' projections with the signs in the heavens that Scripture says will precede Jesus Christ's return. Regardless of what occurs at the next alignment of planets, the Bible clearly prophesies that at the time of Christ's return there will be signs in the heavens. The sun will become hot and bright, the moon will shine as the sun, there will be storms, earthquakes, and related catastrophes.

Then the sun will become dark, and when our solar system is plunged into utter darkness, every eye will see the brightness of Jesus Christ as He comes with the armies of heaven.

The Stars

The prophetic indicators of the last days include signs in the sun, moon, and *stars*. Christians are not stargazers. As believers we should live according to the Word of God. Still, the heavenly bodies are not without significance. We read in Genesis 1:14 that God made them for seasons, days, years, and signs. The Jewish historian Josephus tells us that the sons of Seth studied the heavens to discern God's will. The Egyptians interpreted an alignment of Jupiter and Saturn in the sign of Pisces three years before the birth of Moses as a sign that a great leader would be born among the Jews. Jupiter and Saturn were again in conjunction in the year that Jesus was born—not once, but three times. Had the Magi not been looking at the heavens for a sign, they might never have discerned from God's special star that a king of the Jews had been born.

In February of 1979, the last solar eclipse that will be visible in North America in this century created quite a stir. Many parts of the Pacific Northwest were plunged into darkness for several minutes, and eclipse-watchers as far south as the southeastern United States peered through overcast skies in an attempt to see this exciting phenomenon.

Many people do not realize that several eclipses, both solar and lunar, occur each year in various parts of the world. In fact, the minimum number that can occur in any one year is two. The maximum is seven. In 1917, the year of the signing of the Balfour Declaration, there were seven eclipses. Seven is the divine

The Parade of Planets

number of perfection—God's seal of approval. As the seventh eclipse appeared, General Allenby marched into Jerusalem, thereby putting into effect the agreements contained in the Balfour Declaration.

Another heavenly sign that has held an important meaning for mankind has been the appearance of comets. Comets have always been understood to foreshadow a fall of world rulers. The ancient Bayeux Tapestry shows King Harold in 1066 looking up in dismay at a bright comet. In that year Harold lost both his crown and his life.

From Shakespeare's *Julius Caesar* we read:

> When Beggars die there are
> no comets seen;
> The heavens themselves blaze
> forth the death of princes.

There were seven eclipses in the year 1973, and more bad news for man developed with each additional eclipse. Famine reared its ugly head. World inflation began in earnest. The energy crisis took on new and serious proportions. Another war broke out between Israel and the Arab states, bringing many nations to the brink of war. As the seventh eclipse appeared, Comet Kohoutek came streaking into our solar system like a Roman candle. It sputtered and then died like a match.

It was the opinion of many that Kohoutek was the dud of the century, but it accomplished its purpose as a sign of falling princes. During the eighteen months Kohoutek was in our solar system, all ten leaders of the free world's greatest nations either died or fell from power in political disgrace. A UPI news release that appeared in the May 29, 1974, edition of *The Houston Post* stated in part:

> In 15 short months, all nine leaders of the European Common Market nations have fallen from power. Beginning with the downfall of Irish Premier Pierre Werner's government party, the nine have fallen with a domino-like regularity . . . French President George Pompidou died. West German Chancellor Willy Brandt resigned in a spy scandal. Italian Premier Giulion Andreotti succumbed to parliamentary maneuvering. The others lost elections: Britain's Ted Heath (over strikes), Denmark's Anker Jorgensen (over high taxes) and Holland's Barent Biesheuvel (over high cost of living).

As explained within the context of the article, the leaders of governments in Belgium and Luxembourg also fell from power, and less than three months later, the tenth and highest of all fell. President Nixon resigned in extreme humiliation on August 9, 1974.

Nine in Scripture is the number of rebellion. As stated in *Number in Scripture* by E. W. Bullinger, nine "marks the completeness, the end and issue of all things as to man—the judgment of man and his works." August corresponds to the Jewish month of Av, and both Solomon's Temple and Herod's Temple were destroyed on the ninth day of Av. The fall of the heads of states of the nine leading nations of the free world in relation with the

The Parade of Planets

appearance of Kohoutek, and concluding with the resignation of President Nixon on the ninth of August, appears to be more than coincidental.

The conjunctions of the planets Jupiter and Saturn have traditionally been accepted as the heralds of the birth of kings. In 1982 all nine planets will be in conjunction. Will the coming parade of planets serve as a heavenly banner?

> And I saw heaven opened, and behold a white horse; and he that sat upon him was called Faithful and True, and in righteousness he doth judge and make war.... on his head were many crowns.... And he hath on his vesture and on his thigh a name written, KING OF KINGS, AND LORD OF LORDS (Rev. 19:11,12,16).

NINE
Mark of the Beast

One of the most fascinating aspects of prophetic study is comparing technology's startling advances with the divinely given signs of Christ's second coming. In previous chapters we have touched briefly on several of these advances and their prophetic significance, but in this final chapter we will consider one of them more carefully.

There are many who can clearly remember the first days of the Social Security Administration when, under the Roosevelt administration, U.S. citizens were first issued Social Security numbers. This development worried some thoughtful Bible students. They were fearful that this might be the beginning of the numbering system of the Antichrist:

> And he causeth all, both small and great, rich and poor, free and bond, to receive a mark in their right hand, or in their foreheads: And that no man might buy or sell, save he that had the mark, or the name of the beast, or the number of his name. Here is wisdom. Let him that hath understanding count the

number of the beast: for it is the number of a man; and his number is Six hundred threescore and six (Rev. 13:16–18).

We are firmly convinced that three truths are implicit in this prophecy: (1) Under the Antichrist's system, men will definitely be marked or numbered. (2) That numbering system will not be so obscure as to be impossible for us to understand when it appears. (3) We are to be watching for its appearance.

History has shown that the worried speculations about Social Security numbers being the mark of the Beast were probably unfounded. Granted, there are many who feel that the Social Security system has mushroomed into a beast in its own right, but apparently it isn't the Beast of Revelation 13. Still, we cannot criticize those who first expressed such a concern. They were living in the spirit of the above passage. They were watching. They were keeping an eye on current events in the hope of discerning some sign of Christ's return.

In fact, they may not have been entirely wrong. The Social Security system has made Americans accustomed to being numbered. The concept of being assigned a number by the government that would mark us for the rest of our natural lives was quite frightening to many people several decades ago. Now few if any in our society give the practice a second thought.

Probably the most significant technological advancement on the road to the last days has been the development of the computer. Primitive computers were used in World War II to convert radar information to firing data for antiaircraft artillery and naval guns. The first commercial computer did not appear until 1947, but nothing since the creation of Adam has changed the life of man and the world economy in such a short time.

In just over thirty years, every facet of modern life has been altered by the computer. If every computer in the world were to be shut down suddenly, planes would not fly, trains would not run, traffic lights would not change, banks would have to close, space projects would be aborted, and department stores and grocery stores would have to close. If computers were suddenly silenced, the world would be thrown into chaos.

With this in mind, let us consider the mechanics of enforcing the mark of the Beast for every man, woman, and child in the world. First, there would have to be a universal money system. Second, no coin or currency is mentioned in the business transaction of buying, working, or selling. Third, the Antichrist will not permit any business transaction without the use of the mark or number. Every store, every factory, every bank, every place where buying, working, or selling is practiced will be under the control of the Beast. Thanks to the computer, all of that is now possible.

The educational periodical *Senior Scholastic* recently carried a rather startling article. It predicted that in the future cashless society, an individual computer number would be tattooed on every person's forehead, probably in an ink visible under

Mark of the Beast

ultraviolet light. Recently we asked a banker in Washington, D.C. if he could envision a development where computer numbers would replace cash and checks. He replied that such a system is a possibility and has been predicted by some. However, he hoped it would never come into being, because it would have to be ruthlessly controlled. As long ago as 1973, the December issue of *Smithsonian* magazine editorialized: "Just about everything is changing. We dial direct instead of chatting with an operator. We will certainly go to metric before too long. No doubt, we will soon be precisely numbered members of a cashless society."

An interesting article appeared in the September 21, 1976, *Daily Oklahoman*. Entitled "Cashless Society Expected to Become Reality Soon," it read in part:

> The long-talked-about "cashless society" is almost here. Bank debit cards are expected to go into nationwide use soon.... This [will] eliminate the need for statements, checkwriting, finance charges, envelopes, and postage. Maybe we can learn to get along without money.... Payment of bills by debit card is coming. Computer-coded prices on items at supermarkets and bank debit cards will make it possible for customers to obtain groceries without seeing the money come or seeing it go. Changes are taking place and demanding such rapid adaptation of individuals that a new word has been coined to describe them—rapidation.... Scientists have reduced the size and cost of computers, so that countless uses have developed.

Perhaps one of the most important articles to appear in the popular press was a feature entitled "Coming Soon: Electronic Money," published in the November, 1976 *Reader's Digest.*

> George Johnson, and millions of other senior citizens never see a Social Security check. Their pension payments are deposited into their bank accounts electronically, with no paper changing hands. . . . Nearly one million American workers, including nearly the entire active-duty U.S. Air Force, now have wages or salaries automatically deposited in their bank accounts by means of magnetic tape. Half a million others make regular payments for rents, loans, bills, etc. in the same manner, without signing anything. . . . At the checkout counters of several hundred supermarkets in the United States, no cash or checks need change hands. The clerk simply slips your plastic 'debit' card into an electronic terminal connected by telephone line to the bank's computer, and the cost of your groceries is instantly transferred from your bank account to the store's. Automatic Teller Machines are located in shopping centers, apartment complexes, airports, factories, hospitals, or the outside walls of banks. They will give you your bank balance, issue up to $100 a day from your account, accept cash and checks for deposit, transfer funds between savings, checking and credit accounts, and present you with a printed receipt for each transaction. In Minneapolis you may conduct financial transactions without ever leaving your home. By pushing the proper keys on your touch-tone telephone, you direct a computer in the savings bank to switch funds from your account to the accounts of stores, utilities, etc. . . . On the

back of each card is a magnetic stripe with your PIN number and/or bank account number invisibly micro-encoded. . . . If you make a mistake, the machine will tell you and wait for you to correct it. . . . After each withdrawal, the computer records your new balance, and it will not honor the next transaction made with the card if you are overdrawn or have exceeded a daily limit.

The most interesting statement in the entire article is the closing paragraph:

In this new, totally electronic age, the enforcement of financial obligation will present few difficulties, since failure to pay up could be disastrous. The culprit might even be forced to undergo what EFT men call "plastic surgery"—the cutting off of his bank cards. Economically speaking, this would make him a non-person.

When we first read these words, they seemed to jump off the page—a "non-person," unable to buy or sell. For the first time in history the technology exists to accomplish exactly what Bible prophecy attributes to the Antichrist: control of the world through a stranglehold on world economy. We are not suggesting that computers, in themselves, are evil. We do not believe it is a sin to use the convenient aspects of the newer banking methods. We are not implying that the men who have developed these methods and the computers that make them possible are agents of the Antichrist. We do believe, however, that the system now being instituted, or one very similar to it, will eventually be seized by the Antichrist and used for his diabolical purposes.

Some have asked us, rather fearfully, if using the computer method of buying and selling amounts to taking the mark of the Beast. The answer, of course, is no. As long as we are in the world we have to live by the world's economic standards to some extent. The mark of the Beast will come when the great world dictator sits in the temple in Jerusalem and demands universal worship. However, we believe that according to 1 Thessalonians 4 and 5, Christians will be taken out of the world before this abomination occurs.

TEN

The Last Century

President Valéry Giscard d'Estaing of France has said, "The world is unhappy. It is unhappy because it doesn't know where it is going and because it senses that, if it knew, it would discover that it was heading for disaster."

Henry Kissinger burst into tears before a television camera as he declared, "One has to live with a sense of the inevitability of tragedy."

Albert Schweitzer considered the future thusly: "Man has lost the capacity to foresee and forestall. He will end by destroying the earth."

Every indication is that we are living in the last century of man's history. The appearance of the world's first test-tube baby conjures visions of a latter-day Hitler with dreams of a new, genetically perfect race. Genetic experiments already in process raise the spectre of a new strain of super bacteria, unlike anything ever seen before, that could literally wipe out large portions of the world's population. The optimist can no longer be considered someone who looks on the bright side of world events. The only optimists in today's world, aside from Christians, are those who are not looking at all.

The signs of our time indicate that we are living in the last century. The age is winding down. God does not want us to be ignorant of that day when Christ will call away the believers of the Church Age and plunge the world into those last seven years of terrible tribulation.

But the question of whether or not Christ will come before the end of this century is not the most important question facing us. The most important question is: If Jesus Christ were to return today, would we be ready for His coming? God's promise is that all who have died in the faith of Jesus Christ will rise to meet Him in the air (1 Thess. 4:13–18). Those believers who are alive on that day will rise instantly to meet Jesus in the air and be reunited with the resurrected saints. Then, the Tribulation will begin in earnest.

All God's signs seem to be saying that the day is very near, even at the door. God, however, has provided another door. Jesus said, "I am the door: by me if any man enter in, he shall be saved. . . . I am come that they might have life, and that they might have it more abundantly" (John 10:9,10).

Every person who has not already been born again by faith in Jesus Christ is faced with two choices. He may believe on Jesus Christ, who died for the sins of mankind, and be saved. Or he may reject the message of Christ. To turn from Christ is to risk dying in sin and possibly living to face all the terrors of the Great Tribulation, with its wars,

The Last Century

earthquakes, famine, political and economic upheaval, disease, and misery. To reject Christ is to face all eternity without God and without hope.

The study of prophecy has two major purposes: (1) to encourage those who have trusted Christ to be about the urgent business of bringing people to Christ, and (2) to encourage those who have never trusted Jesus to accept Him as Savior and Lord. Paul wrote,

> If thou shalt confess with thy mouth the Lord Jesus, and shalt believe in thine heart that God hath raised him from the dead, thou shalt be saved. For with the heart man believeth unto righteousness; and with the mouth confession is made unto salvation (Rom. 10:9,10).

We could be living in the last century. In fact, Jesus could call away the believers today. Are you ready?